"Knowing the connection between our faith and ⟨ is not enough. It is too easy to get caught up in tr pointments in our work, without connecting the lives. Denise Daniels and Shannon Vandewarke keep our work rooted in our walk with God. A wo.........ui ,esource for any working Christian—and that's all of us!"

—**Albert Erisman, retired Boeing executive**
**Author of *The Accidental Executive* and *The ServiceMaster Story***

"Eugene Peterson once wrote, 'I'm prepared to contend that the primary location for spiritual formation is the workplace.' Now we finally have a guide for what that actually looks like for those of us living in a busied, fragmented world. Denise Daniels and Shannon Vandewarker have written the authoritative guide to spiritual formation in and through our work. *Working in the Presence of God* will bless, inspire, and give practical insight to anybody wanting to live out the gospel in the day-to-day realities of family, community, and work."

—**Jeff Haanen, CEO**
**Denver Institute for Faith & Work**

"In this remarkable book, spiritual disciplines such as confession, sabbath, lament, and solitude are applied to the workplace. With creative chapters such as "Liturgy of the Commute," Denise Daniels and Shannon Vandewarker challenge us to rethink our approach to work. Placing a spike in the heart of the artificial sacred/secular split, they call us to make Jesus lord over every aspect of our lives."

—**Alec Hill, President Emeritus, InterVarsity Christian Fellowship**
**Author of *Just Business: Christian Ethics in the Marketplace***

"Most Christians I know work a job. Likewise, most Christians I know practice some form of spiritual discipline. But most do not connect the two. Daniels and Vandewarker wrote *Working in the Presence of God* to do just that. Their book is visionary, imaginative, thoughtful, and practical. Never have I thought of lament, for example, as a spiritual discipline that applies to work. Nor have I considered celebrating my professional successes as a legitimate spiritual practice. I found myself both intrigued and engaged from beginning to end. I am already applying it to my daily life. Thanks to the authors for writing such a short, clear, and winsome book."

—**Gerald L. Sittser, Professor of Theology, Whitworth University**
**Author of *Water from a Deep Well* and *Resilient Faith***

"How can a Christian actively practice the presence of God in and through day-to-day work? Many of us in the faith and work movement have been waiting a very long time for exactly this sort of book. It fills a critical gap. Daniels and Vandewarker offer unique insights that are going to be a true gift to pastors and professionals alike for years to come."

—**Matthew Kaemingk, Assistant Professor of Christian Ethics**
**Fuller Theological Seminary**

"In the frantic and fragmented world we live in today, we have lost our ability to reflect deeply and bring real coherence to the rhythms of our lives. This book is both theologically sound and eminently practical, as it helps us recover a liturgy for our working lives. From our morning rituals (such as our commute) through the activities of our days (both joyful and toilsome), to considering new ways to rest and to observe the Sabbath, this is the handbook to bring these practices into reality. A much-needed source code drawn from the pages of Scripture, providing practical guidance for examining and reimagining our daily activity and stories from the field, *Working in the Presence of God* is the missing piece for true faith/work coherence in today's world of work."

**—Lisa Slayton**
**Founder and Principal, Tamim Partners**
**Former CEO, Pittsburgh Leadership Foundation**

"*Working in the Presence of God* is a necessary book. Shannon Vandewarker and Denise Daniels provide us with the most practical guide yet for Christians who want to connect their deepest cares and commitments to their everyday work. I cannot wait to use this book in my workshops and classes—and to recommend it to my friends!"

**—Gideon Strauss, Academic Dean and Associate Professor of Worldview Studies, Institute for Christian Studies, Toronto, Canada**

"What a brilliant and needed addition to the faith and work movement. It is one thing to understand faith and work conceptually, but it is quite another thing to figure out the exact steps we need to take to truly move toward Christ. While this book is practical with providing answers of what we can do during the workweek, it also provides ample theology and background. With more than two-thirds of workers as dissatisfied-to-miserable in America, we need these steps that orient us toward God hour to hour and day to day. This book helps workers experience a heart change that can impact their workplace community and beyond. Kudos to Vandewarker and Daniels for this book—and for helping us move from pontification to practice."

**—Missy Wallace, Executive Director, Nashville Institute for Faith and Work**

"*Working in the Presence of God* offers remarkable insight and encouragement for everyday saints seeking to be faithful in and through the seemingly unremarkable events of daily life. Its accessible teaching, practical exercises, and applicable wisdom offer what amounts to a complete and winsome guidebook for loving God and others through even the most ordinary day job. This book is a gift to the church. I am so glad to know there is finally a resource that brings theology down to the level of a morning commute, a whiteboard session, a construction site—that is, where most of the saints live. This is food for their souls."

**—Kate Harris, former Interim Executive Director, The Fellows Initiative**
**Author of *Wonder Women: Navigating the Challenges of Motherhood, Career, and Identity***

"In addition to the powerful, cogent, and life-giving affirmation of the redemptive potential our work, this book casts fresh vision and hope that our daily activities can be employed in ways that form us into the kind of people we long to be. From our commute to our calendar, this book will help make every moment an ally in our transformation toward Christlikeness."

**—Geoffrey Hsu, Executive Director, Flourish San Diego**

"One of the greatest, yet often overlooked perils of the Sunday-to-Monday gap is the failure to grasp that it is in the seemingly mundane moments of everyday work where we are most spiritually formed. Our work matters not only because it is an essential way we love our neighbor, but it is also a primary way we are spiritually formed. We shape our work and our work shapes us. With timeless insight and down-to-earth guidance, Vandewarker and Daniels beckon apprentices of Jesus to pursue in their places of work the attentive-with-God life. This is a book for which I have been eagerly waiting for a long time. I highly recommend it."

**—Tom Nelson, President, Made to Flourish**
**Author of *Work Matters* and *The Economics of Neighborly Love***

"How can a Christian actively practice the presence of God in and through day-to-day work? Many of us in the faith and work movement have been waiting a very long time for exactly this sort of book. It fills a critical gap. Daniels and Vandewarker offer unique insights that are going to be a true gift to pastors and professionals alike for years to come."

**—Matthew Kaemingk, Assistant Professor of Christian Ethics**
**Fuller Theological Seminary**

"This is an extraordinary book. I mean this literally. It is 'extra-ordinary.' Among many excellent volumes on God and work, this book is unique in its focus on 'spiritual practices' for the workplace. These practices, built on the foundation of Scripture and Christian wisdom, will help you discover God's presence and grow in Christ through your 'everyday work.' You'll know this book offers something exceptional when, in an early chapter called 'Liturgy of Commute,' you learn how to turn drudgery into devotion. *Working in the Presence of God*, perhaps more than any other book relating faith and work, has made a difference in how I actually work, live, and pray. I commend it to you with enthusiasm and gratitude."

**—Mark D. Roberts, Executive Director**
**Max De Pree Center for Leadership, Fuller Theological Seminary**

"The Triune God creates and, as we are made in God's image, Daniels and Vandewarker remind us that God has created us to do good work. But in a world that is fallen yet redeemed through the salvific work of Jesus Christ, God now calls us to redeem work in all life's spheres. The authors provide reflections and spiritual practices for this work in a world where toil is ever present in our own lives and the world around us. They have invited us to develop daily rhythms associated with work as an act of worship."

**—Margaret Diddams, Provost, Wheaton College**

# WORKING
## in the Presence of

# GOD

*Spiritual Practices for Everyday Work*

Denise Daniels
Shannon Vandewarker

HENDRICKSON
PUBLISHERS

THEOLOGY <u>OF</u> WORK ▶ PROJECT

**Working in the Presence of God: Spiritual Practices for Work**

Hendrickson Publishers Marketing, LLC
P. O. Box 3473
Peabody, Massachusetts 01961-3473
www.hendrickson.com

ISBN 978-1-68307-222-5

*Printed in the United States of America*

*First Printing—September 2019*

Library of Congress Control Number: 2019941904

# CONTENTS

**Preface:** A Theological Framework                                    xi

**Introduction:** The Ordinary Rhythm of Work                           1

**Part One: Orienting to Work**

1. Liturgy of Commute                                                  21

2. Workplace as Holy Ground                                            37

3. Surrendering the Calendar                                           48

4. Reading Scripture at Work                                           64

**Part Two: Engaging in Work**

5. Affirmation of Calling                                              83

6. Gratitude and Celebration                                          104

7. Confession at Work                                                 121

8. Lamenting Work                                                     135

**Part Three: Reflecting on Work**

9. Solitude: Alone in God's Presence                                  151

10. Prayer of Examen for Work                                         166

11. Sabbath: Ceasing from Work                                        187

**Epilogue:** Paying Attention to God on a
Lifelong Journey                                                      205

**Bibliography**                                                      207

**Notes**                                                             209

# PREFACE

## *A Theological Framework for Work*

In Genesis 1 and 2, one of the first things we learn is that God is a worker.[1] In the beginning, God is a light bringer, an ocean spreader, a land former, and a star inventor. The creation is not finished in an instant, but God works to make these things come to be. After the heavens and the earth are created, God's final act of creative work is to make human beings out of dust and fill them with the breath from his very own lungs.

Next, God gives Adam and Eve work to do. It's important to note that the mandate for work comes *before* things go sideways in Eden—*before* their fall and subsequent banishment (Gen. 2:15). Made in the image and likeness of God—the *imago Dei*—Adam and Eve have work to do that connects with God's purposes for the world. Genesis 2 suggests that God himself takes care of the plants before there is someone to work the ground (Gen. 2:4–5). When Adam is created, Eden gains a human gardener. Although God could have created a fully developed world, he waited in order to provide someone else the joy of being a caretaker, a co-creator, a worker.

God provided work to do and then commanded Adam and Eve to fill the earth and to subdue it, meaning that they were to make something of the world. As Timothy Keller and Katherine Leary

Alsdorf suggest, "The word 'subdue' indicates that, though all God had made was good, it was still to a great degree undeveloped. God left creation with deep untapped potential for cultivation that people were to unlock in their labor."[2] God had created the earth, but it was not finished. He got everything started and then told humans he was going to use them to be co-creators in filling the earth, working to make it grow and flourish.

## CO-CREATORS WITH GOD

Like an empty lot in need of building plans, construction, and landscaping, God gave Adam and Eve the garden and the created order to develop. They were told to work the land and cultivate the dirt so that it would bear fruit. They too were to bear the fruit of making a family and creating the first human culture.

As we look at the beginning of creation, we see our original purpose. As Adam and Eve were called to subdue the earth, we are also humans created in God's image, called to work as co-creators with the Lord of creation. We are to make something with the materials we are given. But more importantly, God asks us to make something of the world in such a way that it reflects the *imago Dei—his* image.

When we work, we not only reflect the image of the original Creator, but we also accomplish this work through the power and movement of God expressed through us. Just as Adam and Eve could not have accomplished their work without the Lord's aid, we too find our best fulfillment through work done that aligns with God's purposes and that recognizes God's empowerment. As humans with agency, we do not throw up our hands and leave all the work to our heavenly Father, nor do we put all the pressure on ourselves to conjure up meaning, success, and progress in our work. We are called to be *co-creators*. In that co-creation, we follow the call of God to cultivate and subdue by showing up, taking responsibility for our work, and doing it to the best of our abilities. We do all this in the knowledge that we can do nothing without the enabling power of God working through us, as we experience the privilege of continuing the good work he began at creation.

## THE WONDER OF WORK[3]

### *Work Is Good*

Revisiting the creation story reveals God's attitude as he worked. It was not in drudgery that God swirled planets into existence and flung them onto their orbital paths. The Lord did not begrudgingly put together atoms and chemicals to make water flow into the oceans. No, the Creator of the universe delighted in his work, calling creation *tove mode*[4] (Gen. 1:31 in the Hebrew), which can be translated as "overflowingly abundant" and "ever increasing in good." God called creation "abundantly good," because he worked to create it and it brought him great delight.

The pinnacle of God's creation was humanity, and the Lord was pleased with the work he performed in bringing humanity to life. God's work is indeed delightful! As his image-bearers, we have been created also to delight in the work God has given us to do. Yes, to be sure, some things are frustrating and heartbreaking about our work. But this is not a result of God's original intent and design for the work he gave us. We are not given work to do begrudgingly, but to find delight in it. Joy can be found in our work, because we have the privilege of being in relationship with the Creator of the universe who gives us the responsibility to co-create alongside the Trinity, making something of our little corners of the world.

## THE HEARTBREAK OF WORK

### *Work Is Good, But It's Broken*

As anyone who has engaged in any sort of work knows, it is not always delightful. While the original intent of work was to create and produce with joy, if we are honest, there are parts of our labor that break our hearts, that frustrate us to no end, and that we do not understand. Relationships in our workplaces can be flawed or even destructive. The reality of our work is that there is often toil involved in it. It is sometimes hard and can bring deep disappointment and sorrow, and our efforts do not always result in the outcomes we intended or desired. The residue of the forbidden fruit is smeared all over our workplaces—and not surprisingly, many experience institutional brokenness on daily basis.

This, of course, cañ be frustrating and deeply discouraging. In our exasperation, we groan with all of creation that things sometimes do not work as they should, problems are not solved as quickly as we would like, and we do not accomplish what we had hoped. So, the ache of creation we feel in our work reminds us that we labor in a fallen world—a world that does not function as it was intended. Keller and Alsdorf describe our condition well, "While God blessed work to be a glorious use of our gifts and his resources to prosper the world, it is also cursed because of mankind's fall. Work exists now in a world sustained by God but disordered by sin."[5]

## THE HOPE OF WORK

### *Work Is Good, but It's Broken—and Christ Is the One Who Can Redeem It*

And yet, in the midst of the brokenness of our work, there is hope—hope that Christ enters into our work and shows up not only as the redeemer of all humanity but as the redeemer of all of creation, including our work. We long for the day when Christ will make all things new. We hope for that day, certainly, but we also know that Jesus' presence goes with us into fallen places bringing redemption, restoration, and hope. We are people who live in the "already" and the "not yet" of redemption.

In Christ's promise of restoration, each day is an opportunity for us to witness his presence, bringing redemption to our work, our workplaces, and to those with whom we work. In Christ, frustration can be turned into creative energy for a new project. In Christ, conflicts can become grounds for reconciliation. In Christ, what was cracked in our work is mended and made new. The pervasive nature and power of sin is turned back on itself through the power of redemption. As far as sin has affected humanity and creation, Christ's redemptive power goes farther, seeking to reconcile all of humanity and creation to God.

There is an ancient Japanese art called *kintsugi* in which once-broken glasses, plates, and bowls are taken and repaired using a fine gold adhesive. These pieces, though, are not just repaired. They are seen as more beautiful for having been broken. In fact, "The *kintsugi* method conveys a philosophy not of replacement, but of awe, reverence, and restoration. The gold-filled cracks of a once-broken item are a testament to its history."[6]

This ancient art is an image of what Christ's redemption brings to fallen creation. It is not only repaired but reflects the beauty of God in the process. It may be hard to see Christ's work of redemption in our work, especially when so much of it feels so broken and not as it should be. But just because we don't recognize it, this doesn't mean God is not working to redeem.

This is why spiritual practices are so important to our working lives. *Spiritual practices open our eyes and tune our ears to where we may have missed God working.*

In using the spiritual practices outlined in this book, we pray that through the power of the Holy Spirit, you may see better where God is at work in your work, and that you will join him in new ways, co-creating for the redemption of the workplace where God has placed you.

## WORK IN THE NEW CREATION

### *Work Is Good, but It's Broken, Christ Is the One Who Can Redeem It—and He Will Make It Fully Restored in the "New Heaven and New Earth" (Rev. 21:1)*

Many people have the misconception that work is just a part of this life. Those who think this may assume they just need to put in their time, and then they will be finally free of work when they die. This view does not take into consideration a robust theology of work. If God's original intent was that work was created as good—and even delightful—then why would it end? Longing for the end of work could bring hope to someone who is stuck in the drudgery of toilsome work, but it is actually not a biblical concept. The intent of God is that we will continue to work in the new creation. In the end, God will usher in a new heaven and a new earth—a place bursting with culture and life.

This means that in the end, our resurrection will not be just for our souls, but it will be for our bodies as well—just as it was with Jesus. The scriptural view of the new heavens and earth is of a physical and real place. On Christ's return, the saved will be ushered into a new reality: The new heaven and earth will involve our bodies and the things of creation, including our work, in a resurrected, fully redeemed, and restored form. As Darrell Cosden says in his book, *The Heavenly Good of Earthly Work,*

> Both as city and as Jerusalem, the new creation is a transformed and now holy place. The vision (in Revelation) suggests that God is pleased to gather up, transform, and include not just his "pure" creation, but also the genuine additions to the created reality that we have brought about through creation-transforming actions.[7]

Redeemed bodies and redeemed work? How can this be? Andy Crouch explains it this way:

Just as we hope and expect to be bodily present, in bodies we cannot now imagine yet that we believe will be recognizably our own—just as the disciples met Jesus in a resurrected body that had unimaginable capabilities yet was recognizably his own—it seems clear from Isaiah 60 and from Revelation 21 that we will find the new creation furnished with culture. Cultural goods too will be transformed and redeemed, yet they will be recognizably what they were in the old creation—or perhaps more accurately they will be what they always could have been. The New Jerusalem will be truly a city: a place suffused with culture, a place where culture has reached its full flourishing. It will be the place where God's instruction to the first human beings is fulfilled, where all the latent possibilities of the work will be discovered and released by creative, cultivating people.[8]

The good news about work is that God gave us good work to do: work we will continue to cultivate—in a fulfilled and redeemed form—into eternity!

# INTRODUCTION

## *The Ordinary Rhythm of Work*

### THE IMPORTANCE OF THE ORDINARY

Scripture is replete with the ordinary—and sadly, we regularly miss it. By looking for the "spiritual" message, we miss the bulk of the text. The "sacred" has been divorced from the "secular," and in the process, we have lost the celebration of the ordinary.

In order to understand why we think and live this way—that God is somehow outside of our everyday, ordinary lives—we need to go back to Greek philosophy, particularly Gnosticism. A common belief held by the Greeks was that the spiritual was much more important than the physical. In fact, the physical world was viewed as evil, whereas the spiritual world was held to be sacred. People were seen not as a body with a soul, but as a soul trapped in a body. Those with means would have slaves do the mundane work necessary for life, while they themselves devoted their time to the life of the mind.

Early Christian communities absorbed this Greek way of thinking to such a degree that gnostic teachers insisted Jesus must not really have had a physical body. They suggested that in order to understand the mystery of the gospel, one needed to reject the physical world and focus on the spiritual. The apostle Paul spills quite a bit of ink pushing back against this heresy in his New Testament letters.

Nonetheless, the Greek dichotomy between the sacred and secular took root; and by the Middle Ages, the division between the spiritual and the physical was further perpetuated with the rise of the monasteries. Those who had a "calling" could separate themselves from regular life in order to devote their time to God. Christians in the West today are the descendants of this way of thinking. In many of our churches, we receive an implicit message that those who are pursuing full-time Christian ministry—missionaries, pastors, or parachurch workers—are doing "God's work" while everyone else is doing "secular work," which is somehow not quite as important. We are living in the midst of a great sacred/secular divide.

But Scripture doesn't split life into sacred and secular. When we look closer at the Bible—examining the stories in the Old Testament, in Jesus' life, and throughout the New Testament—we see something about how God works that we often forget: God knows the power of the ordinary. God very much resides in the everyday nature of our ordinary and sometimes mundane lives.

In Scripture, we see God using common things—such as bushes and fire, water and bread, employers, and the menial place of servants—to reveal himself. He used people's workplaces and children. He used walking sticks and wrestling matches. He used baby bassinets and mothers' compassion. He used cooking pots and olive oil. He used the "stuff" of life to speak.

Then there is Jesus himself. He did miracles with water and wine. He used saliva to heal, and his hands as a balm for sickness. He wrote in the dust to make his point. He used dirt and spit to make mud and reveal the extraordinary in the ordinary. Jesus came into homes to eat and sleep. He walked with fishermen and used their fish to teach them. He used CEOs and lawyers and CPAs in his kingdom. He met women at their most common place—the well—the twenty-first-century equivalent of the kitchen sink.

We gloss over these seemingly insignificant details too often. And when we do, we miss what God is doing, what he is saying. We look for the spiritual message, for something that will feed our souls, when all along God is saying, "I'm here! I'm in the physical, the ordinary elements. Look deeper. I care about these things." As Dallas Willard in his book *The Divine Conspiracy* observed, we live in a "God-bathed world."[1] Indeed we do!

The ordinary is not just something we exist *in* but is something we are called *into*. Embracing our ordinary lives means embracing our actual lives—lives lived with monotony and routine, ordinary moments, and mundane tasks. Embracing the ordinary can be a catalyst for experiencing and being used by God in some deeply profound ways.

In our technologically connected world, we have the perverse opportunity to work frantically all the time. This can become exhausting, and the temptation may be to seek solitude to read Scripture and pray—perhaps a place outside, by the lake or in the mountains, away from our ordinary, everyday existence. While there is nothing wrong with communing with God in quiet and beautiful places, such spaces don't tend to be where most of our everyday lives are lived. As a result of thinking that we need to escape the regularity of our lives to experience God, we perpetuate our own personal division between the sacred and secular, and we may even minimize our engagement with spiritual practices.

By embracing our ordinary lives for what they are, we can find ourselves called to something different. If frantic, never-ending work is one end of the spectrum and a contemplative quiet life is on the other spectrum, then we believe there is a third way. It is the way of becoming attentive to God in the *midst* of the work, in the *midst* of ordinary life. If God cared enough to show up at wells and in mud, then certainly he can show up in spreadsheets, commutes, meetings, and performance reviews. In fact, God is present in hard manual labor, in classrooms, and in dingy convenience stores. Remember that the Creator is the author of work; so whatever your work is, the Lord can communicate to you, use you, and transform you in the midst of it.

About this third way, Tish Harrison Warren, author of *Liturgy of the Ordinary: Sacred Practices in Everyday Life*, says,

> I need a third way—neither frantic activity nor escape from the workaday world, a way of working that is shaped by being blessed and sent. This third way is marked by freedom from compulsion and anxiety because it's rooted in benediction—God's blessing and love, but it also actively embraces God's mission in the world into which we are sent.[2]

It is not a new concept to interact with God throughout our days, finding ourselves sent into our work in the power God. While this may be something to which contemporary Christians are awakening, interacting with God through spiritual practices in our work is actually an ancient concept.

Brother Lawrence was someone who stumbled on the power of entering into the ordinary and now is well known for what he discovered. Brother Lawrence was a Benedictine monk who lived in the 1600s; and through drudgery, his theology of work began to be shaped.

Brother Lawrence was a cook in the monastery kitchen— mundane work he despised at first. While Lawrence was still a young man, God began to transform the monotony of his kitchen into a space where his prayer and work began to intertwine, where the daily act of peeling potatoes became a call to prayer. This time of talking with God, as he labored in the kitchen, became the heart of Brother Lawrence's work. God did this in spite of Brother Lawrence's personal description of being someone who was "a clumsy oaf who broke everything."[3] The phrase he meditated on and became shaped by was the Benedictine motto of *ora et labora* meaning "pray and labor"—or "pray and work."

By using spiritual practices in the workplace, we begin to be attentive to the ways in which God is already present—speaking and acting. Whether you find your work mundane or interesting, physical or intellectual, by incorporating spiritual practices into your daily working rhythms, you too can be shaped by God's transforming hand.

Our hope is that through engaging in the practices in this book, you will find yourself living out the exercise of *ora et labora*—pray and work. We hope your everyday work will become a form of prayer, incarnated and offered to God as a pleasing sacrifice.

When engaged in regularly, these practices can enable you to be more attentive to your work, to the people with whom you work, and to God himself, who cares deeply about all of it. In this attentiveness, may we become people who say, "Lord, I offer my work as my prayer, and my prayer as my work."[4]

## THE PURPOSE OF SPIRITUAL PRACTICES

Formation of the Christian is the goal of living a life of discipleship. Christ doesn't call us simply to accept that the Lord is God and that Christ saved us from our sins. He also desires for us to be formed into his likeness (2 Cor. 3:18). We are to be *daily* transformed into who Christ created us to be. Much of this transformation happens when we pay attention to what God is doing in and around us, and then join in that work.

But, as anyone who has tried to kick a bad habit by sheer willpower knows, we can't change ourselves. We are steeped too deeply in sin that pervades the recesses of all of creation (Rom. 8:3). So merely engaging in a few practices in and of themselves *will not change us*. If we engage these practices with such an attitude, then we run the risk of being just like the Pharisees—wanting to gain the favor of God merely by following the right rules.

We believe that, while engaging in spiritual practices is incredibly important for the lives of the followers of Christ, engaging and orienting our lives and our work rhythms around these practices will not by themselves transform us. As Paul reminds us "We neither make nor save ourselves" (Eph. 2:7 The Message). If we engage in spiritual practices with the hope that they can change us, then our efforts will be futile. But if we engage in these practices with the knowledge that it is *God* who is forming us through them—that it is not up to *us* to transform ourselves—then they can be incredible tools, whereby we open ourselves to God's power.

We can plan out a whole liturgy for work, implementing practices throughout our work week; but if this liturgy is done with the wrong attitude, then our efforts will amount to nothing. As Kyle David Bennett says in his book *Practices of Love*,[5] God comes down harshly on those who outwardly practice piety and yet inwardly are not changed, because their focus is on their own efforts toward holiness (Isa. 58).

Paul speaks of this in Ephesians: We are the workmanship *of God* (Eph. 2:10). That means, we don't create ourselves or transform ourselves. But the verse goes on: We are the workmanship of God, created *to do good works*. This means we will work differently as a result of being in relationship with God, the master worker. We will treat our coworkers differently, and we will be transformed, in love, to love those around us.

The point of spiritual practices is to be made into the likeness of Christ, *for the sake of our neighbor*. Yes, we may come to know God in deeper ways by reading Scripture in the workplace, by establishing a liturgy for our commute, or through surrendering our calendar to God. But if these disciplines are merely for the sake of knowing intellectually more about God or for experiencing more of God ourselves, then we have missed the point. As Kristen Deede Johnson observes:

> Whether we are praying or fasting, keeping the Sabbath or remaining in solitude, we have the extraordinary gift of never having to rely on our own strength, commitment, or passion. Whether we are aware of it or not, God is the one prompting us, the one interceding for us, the one receiving and sanctifying what we offer, and the one sanctifying *us* through the whole process. *It's not the disciplines themselves but God at work through them that enables us to love him and love our neighbor more and more.*[6]

## BECOMING AWARE OF THE RHYTHM OF WORK

In order to engage in spiritual practices at work, you first have to become aware of the rhythms of your work. Of course, these rhythms will be different if you are a teacher rather than a corporate manager, or a medical professional rather than a truck driver. Regardless of your work, however, there is a rhythm and pattern to it. These cadences might vary day to day or week to week, and you might be able to discern them over the season of a school year or the season of a fiscal year. These patterns might be regular and clear, or they might vary wildly. Whatever your job, the first step in engaging in spiritual practices at work is for you to become aware of the rhythms of your specific work.

Many times, we are not aware of our own working patterns. We go to work and perform the same duties or functions over and over, but we never really pay attention to what we are doing, or even if we are doing them repeatedly.

Paying attention and becoming aware of how you go about your day is the gateway to exploring and engaging spiritual practices at work in a meaningful way. These practices are not meant to be viewed as just one more task to add to your to do list but are rather to be incorporated into the fabric of your working day and week. Without recognizing the rhythm of your work, you will not know where you can implement a practice in a given part of your work. The cadence of your work can be found in your daily schedule, the order of your tasks,, and whatever you do repeatedly throughout the day or the week.

For example, the daily tasks of a hospital nurse might include the following:

- *Commute to work*

- *Check in at nurse station*

- *Meet with charge nurse and nursing team*

- *Get nursing report from previous nurse*

- *Look up patient information*
- *Make a plan for the day*
- *Wash hands*
- *Enter patient's exam room*
- *Engage with patient*
- *Do head-to-toe assessment*
- *Chart assessment*
- *Reposition patient to prevent skin breakdown*
- *Clean patient*
- *Help with morning routine, change patient gown, change linens, brush patient's teeth, wash patient's face*
- *Organize room and resupply room if needed*
- *Check morning vital signs*
- *Answer family questions*
- *Answer patient questions*
- *Administer medicine or complete medical procedures*
- *Get patient out of bed to walk hallway or to be up in the chair for breakfast*
- *Check blood sugar if needed*
- *Help patient with breakfast*
- *Visit other patients to perform the same tasks*
- *Give report to doctors during rounds*
- *Talk with doctors about the needs of a given patient*
- *Bring up any patient concerns or questions about medical care with the doctors*

- *Do physical assessment, check vitals, chart for each patient*
- *Administer medications*
- *Ambulate hallway with each patient as able*
- *Get patients up to chair for lunch, help with feeding*
- *Eat lunch*
- *Check labs if needed*
- *Administer blood if needed*
- *Coordinate patient care with the physical therapist, occupational therapist, nutritionist, medical team, different specialists*
- *Do patient and family teaching*
- *Answer call lights*
- *Meet with the charge nurse*
- *Train others working at the clinic or on their floor*
- *Help other nurses with their tasks*
- *Answer e-mails*
- *Write and chart shift summary for each patient*
- *Give report to oncoming nurse*
- *Commute home*

The weekly rhythm of a midlevel manager might include:

- *Commute to work*
- *Enter office space*
- *Check morning items and create to-do list*
- *Check e-mails*

- *Morning meeting with team*
- *Answer e-mails*
- *Problem solving session with team members*
- *Midlevel manager meeting*
- *Lunch meeting*
- *Project planning time*
- *Answer e-mails*
- *Employee review or one-on-one meeting*
- *Summarize action items and schedule new meetings*
- *Commute home*

A sample of a work rhythm for a teacher might include:

- *Commute to work*
- *Engage in staff meeting*
- *Get classroom set for the day*
- *Review lesson plans*
- *Greet students as they arrive*
- *Present morning lessons/classes*
- *Eat lunch with teacher team*
- *Present afternoon lessons/classes*
- *Respond to student questions*
- *Say goodbye to students*
- *Answer e-mails*
- *Check in as needed with students or parents*
- *Check in with grade-level teaching team*

- *Prep for the next day*
- *Commute home*

A sample work rhythm for a stay-at-home parent might include:

- *Wake children (or perhaps be woken by them)*
- *Get children ready for the day*
- *Prepare and eat breakfast*
- *Wash dishes and clean up breakfast*
- *Put kids in the car*
- *Outing or errands*
- *Lunch*
- *Naptime*
- *Laundry*
- *Housework*
- *Play with children*
- *Read to children*
- *Clean up after children*
- *Dinner prep, meal, clean-up*
- *Bath time*
- *Reading time*
- *Put children to bed*
- *Prepare for the following day*
- *Relax*
- *Sleep*

Finally, a sample work rhythm for a machinist or manual laborer might include:

- *Commute to work*
- *Clock in*
- *Morning safety and status meeting*
- *Review work orders for the day with supervisor*
- *Begin work order*
- *Complete work order, deliver to next process, order material for next job*
- *Begin next work order*
- *Break*
- *Complete work order, deliver to next process, order material for next job*
- *Empty scrap bins, begin next work order*
- *Lunch*
- *Complete work order, deliver to next process, order material for next job*
- *Begin next work order*
- *Break*
- *Complete work order, deliver to next process, order material for next day*
- *Clean up machines, empty scrap bins, perform preventive maintenance, prepare for next day*
- *Clock out*
- *Commute home*

As you can see, people have different work rhythms, and likely none of the examples above fully describes your own daily or weekly pattern. But all of us have a cadence of work. By becoming aware of these patterns, you can begin to see where in your day the practices in this book might be implemented.

## WORK RHYTHM EXERCISE

To help you become more aware of your own work rhythm, we encourage you to engage in the guided activity on the following pages. Write down your work routines and tasks, and the people with whom you engage in those routines and tasks. If your work changes by the day of the week, you could fill this out for several different days of the week, paying close attention to the common routines which take place daily, and the common routines you engage with on a weekly, rather than daily, basis.

### Orienting to Work

How do you get to work? Do you have a routine once you've entered into your workplace? How do you begin your workday? Do you turn on a computer or other machine? Do you check in with a particular person? Do you make coffee or have breakfast? Write down these routines, tasks, and people:

1.

2.

3.

4.

5.

6.

7.

8.

## *Engaging in Work*

What tasks does your actual work entail? Do you have regular activities, meetings, interactions, or deadlines during the workweek? Do you have a break or lunch at a particular time each day? What reoccurring projects do you participate in? What people do you see with on a regular basis at work? Write down these routines, tasks, and people:

1.

2.

3.

4.

5.

6.

7.

8.

9.

10.

## *Reflecting on Work*

Do you have a routine for ending the workday and exiting your workplace? What types of tasks do you do to prepare for the next day's work? Are there built-in times for reviewing your work and gaining feedback from a supervisor? Write down these routines, tasks, and people:

1.

2.

3.

4.

5.

As you can see, the bulk of your day is likely spent in the "Engaging at Work" section. But "Orienting to Work" and "Reflecting on Work" are deeply important as well. As you read through the different sections of the book, you will want to refer back to this exercise, so be sure to complete it before moving on. Knowing your own work rhythms can help you identify where in your workday or workweek you can incorporate the different spiritual practices we will be discussing throughout the book.

## THE FORMAT OF THIS BOOK

At this point, you may be skeptical about how you might incorporate spiritual practices into your line of work, and that's okay. What we want you to know is that whether you drive a truck or work with incredibly dangerous chemicals, whether you work in a corporate office setting or in a classroom, whether you work as a cleaner or as a caretaker in a hospital or a manufacturing plant, applying some of the practices in this book can transform you, your work, and your relationship with God, through the power of God changing you.

While there are a variety of vocations to which these practices can be applied, there are also different types of unpaid vocations where these practices can be utilized. Nearly everyone works, whether you receive a paycheck or not. What we consider "work" is *that which God has called you to do for his glory, in a particular place and time, for the sake of loving those around you.* So, whether you are paid for your work or not—if you are a stay-at-home parent, a retiree who volunteers, an adult child who cares for an elderly parent, someone looking for employment, or a student—this book is for you. These practices can benefit you and through the power of the Holy Spirit make you more and more into the person God created you to be.

The work you do, the setting where you do it, and the particular culture of your workplace will be different from the next person. Our hope is that no matter what type of work you participate in each day, these practices may be incorporated and adjusted to fit you, your work rhythm, and your workplace. Because everyone's work is a bit different, we have laid out the practices in three sections based on a pattern of work, rather than on the tasks of the work. As you may recognize from the "Rhythm of Work exercise," the sections are: "Orienting to Work," "Engaging in Work," and "Reflecting on Work."

# PART ONE

# Orienting to Work

In this section, we explore where and how you begin your work. For many people, this involves a commute. For others, this involves entering a workspace at home. In most cases, you have a predictable routine you go through when you enter into your workplace. These times of commute and regular routines are not to be dismissed as unimportant.

How we enter our work sets the tone for our awareness of God's presence throughout the workday and week. By paying attention to the way we begin work, we begin the habit of paying attention to where God might be at work throughout our day. Although we often miss this, if we look at Scripture, we see how much God esteems beginnings.

In the Old Testament, how and when people (and God) start something holds significance. People set up monuments, making declarations of new beginnings (Gen. 38:48–50). God outlines when festivals and holy days are to begin and end. The Lord marks out events for the people with starting dates and ending dates (Exod. 12:17–20; Lev. 19:23–25). God sets aside times when battles begin, when holy projects begin, and when times of remembrance begin (Deut. 20:1–4; 1 Kings 5:13–18; 2 Chron. 2:1). Through fasting (Deut. 9:18–20), songs (Deut. 31:19–21; 2 Chron. 29:27–30), and prayer (Lam. 2:19), the Israelites marked the beginning of their interactions with God and days of remembrance.

In the New Testament, we see beginnings as a reflection of God making all things new—a fresh start in Christ. The imminence of the kingdom of God begins with the coming of Christ (Matt. 4:23–25), and it is in that new kingdom that all new beginnings are reflected, *even* the start of a new workday. In God's presence to us now, through Christ, we can trust that mercy and grace will meet us each morning, because God's compassions never fail (Lam. 3:22–23). Each beginning is a chance to experience God's favor and an opportunity to bless those we encounter.

Although some people begin their work in the afternoon or evening, the same principle rings true. Anytime there is a new beginning—whether the start of a day or the start of another shift of work—God's presence, kingdom, mercy, and grace are yours to receive and to be formed by as you go about your work.

In the next few chapters, we will explore four spiritual practices focused on "Orienting to Work."

1. **Liturgy of Commute.** *When you commute to work, you most likely take a similar route each day. This practice involves using landmarks and certain cross streets as the prompts for a liturgy of work.*

2. **Workplace as Holy Ground**. *Think about the place where you do your work as a place of Holy Ground. If God met Moses in the burning bush as he was tending his sheep—a shepherd's workplace—then God can meet you in your workplace as well, whatever that space might be.*

3. **Surrendering the Calendar**. *In this practice, we hold our to-do lists lightly and ask God for his to-do list for us today. One way you can do this is by praying through a to-do list or a calendar before you start work.*

4. ***Reading Scripture in Your Workplace****. Reading Scripture in your work or office space can dramatically change not only how you read Scripture, but also how you go about your work. Seeing God's word in the context in which you work will change how you work, how you interact with your coworkers, and how you are formed by God in the workplace.*

# 1

# LITURGY OF COMMUTE

The daily habits of our lives shape us, whether we are aware of it or not. Often it is those habits we are not aware of that have the most power to mold who we are, how we think, what we buy, and how we interact with others. One of our goals with this book is to encourage you to be as intentional as possible with the routines in your life in order to orient you toward God's purposes. These spiritual practices—or disciplines—can be applied in the everyday ordinary experiences of life and will change what you notice and what becomes important to you. Ultimately, these practices are one of the ways God can change your heart. As James K. A. Smith says, "Discipleship, we might say, is a way to curate your heart, to be attentive to and intentional about what you love."[1] And this intentionality can begin at the start of the day, as you go to work.

How you get to work is important. Not whether you drive or walk, take the bus or ride your bike. Not even the particular route you take. Rather, what happens *in* you while you are getting to work can prepare you for the ways you are attentive to God the rest of the day. Your commute to work, whether it is five minutes or an hour, shapes who you are. So how you go about your commute is deeply important to your working life. If before you get to work you are focused on the frustration, stress, or boredom of the commute, then this will affect how you orient to your work during the day. On the other hand, you can be intentional with your time as you travel, paying attention to God's activity along the way. Your commute can become a type of liturgy and a time when your heart is stirred by God's perspective and purposes.

Think about your commute. What emotions does your experience of traveling to work invoke in you? Does it bring a sense of dread? Hope? Monotony? Is it something you look forward to or a necessary evil in your working life? Maybe there are people you encounter on your way whom you see on a regular basis—a bus driver or fellow passenger, a neighbor, a coworker traveling the same route, or perhaps the person getting coffee from the espresso stand you frequent. What emotions do you feel as you think about these people?

These emotions shape your day, often without your awareness. Let me give an example. For five years, I (Shannon) commuted an hour and a half each way to work in Southern California. My commute came with a sense of dread each day as I woke up early to try to beat the rush-hour traffic to my office. As I drove, my stress levels would rise as I saw the red sea of brake lights up ahead and as my car slowed to a creep on the freeway. Most of the time, I found my commute to be a necessary evil, which prevented me from starting my day productively. I usually passed the time by listening to a local radio show. For the most part, this was an effort to be entertained while driving—and to prevent myself from dying from boredom on yet another freeway drive.

Over time, though, I found that my attitude, desire, and thinking were influenced by the radio station I listened to each day, along with the cacophony of the traffic around me. The patter of the radio hosts interspersed with pop music created a background soundtrack to my commute that was neither restful nor productive. When I noticed myself thinking, it was about the ins and outs of the various relationships of the fictional characters on the TV shows the hosts had talked about. None of this was necessarily bad, but over weeks and months my commute changed me. My mind was being trained to listen inattentively to the noise, my heart was being molded to disengage, and my body was sedentary for three hours each day.

While the level of stress I carried during that season was not exclusively the result of the commute, it certainly contributed to it. By the time I arrived at work, I was often feeling frazzled, tired, and not at all prepared for the work God had for me that day. The commute was something I could not get around. It was a fact of my working life. But the way I allowed the commute to form me was up to me, even though I did not know it at the time.

Your commute is shaping you whether you know it or not. How you begin your day will affect how you go about your work. Will it be *the* determining factor in how your day will go? Probably not. But your commute holds the potential for being an activity through which you can hear from, interact with, and be formed by God. If your commute brings a sense of dread, stress, or anxiety, know this: It doesn't have to. God can redeem your commute to be a time in your day where you are oriented toward his love and prepared to be attentive to the promptings of the Holy Spirit. Beginning your day with an awareness of the Lord's presence can help you live out God's purposes at work.

## EXAMPLES IN SCRIPTURE

A liturgy of commute can be a practice through which you enter into worship of God and seek to hear instructions from the Lord about the day ahead. Throughout Scripture, we see examples of God's people engaging in this. In the book of Deuteronomy, as the Hebrew people are about to enter the Promised Land, the Lord reminds them of what he has done for them, reminds them of his commands, and then instructs them:

> These commandments that I give you today are to be on your hearts. Impress them on your children. Talk about them when you sit at home and when you walk along the road, when you lie down and when you get up. Tie them as symbols on your hands and bind them on your foreheads. Write them on the doorframes of your houses and on your gates. (Deut. 6:6–9)

Did you catch that? *"When you walk along the road."* Of course, walking was their prime mode of transportation. The Lord is saying, "When you live your life and go about your day, including your commute, remember what I have told you. Pay attention to what I have for you, so that you flourish!" God tells the people of Israel how to live the best possible life, and part of it includes engaging with God as they travel—even with young children.

When Jerusalem became the center of worship for the Hebrew people, they took their yearly pilgrimage to the temple there to celebrate the Passover. This travel time was often done in groups, and on the trip the people practiced a travel liturgy of sorts. We know this because several psalms (Pss. 120–134) are subtitled "A Psalm of Ascent," which indicated that these were traveling songs the people sang as they journeyed up Mount Zion to the city. As they went up the mountain, they sang together of God's goodness, sought forgiveness, and called to God for help. These psalms made up their liturgy of commute.

Notice how many references to the travel landscape occur in these psalms. You can imagine that as the travelers passed a given mountain, or when the city gates came into view, it prompted the singing of a particular psalm that reflected a physical feature, describing a trajectory of the landscape. For example, Psalm 121 begins with "I lift up my eyes to the mountains." This might have been sung as the people began the long and tiring trek up the path that led to the city and the temple. They were likely looking at the mountain in front of and around them as they began the climb. When they arrived at the outskirts of the city, you can imagine them singing Psalm 122, which includes the line, "Our feet are standing in your gates, Jerusalem. . . . May there be peace within your walls. . . . I will seek your prosperity."

Once in the city, they would look at the mountains around them and sing Psalm 125, "As the mountains surround Jerusalem, so the LORD surrounds his people." When approaching the temple in the middle of the city, you might have heard them singing Psalm 132:

"Let us go to his dwelling place, let us worship at his footstool." And once they were in the temple, perhaps they sang Psalm 134: "Lift up your hands in the sanctuary and praise the LORD." Throughout the trip, they worshiped; and what they saw around them along the way prompted a different emphasis in their worship. They were practicing a liturgy of commute.

In the New Testament, we see a brief picture of the practice when after Jesus' death and resurrection two of his followers are walking from Jerusalem to the village of Emmaus. Along the way, "They were talking with each other about everything that had happened" (see Luke 24:13–35), including the reports about the empty tomb. A man joins them in their journey and asks what they are talking about. The man eventually explains to them "what was said in all the Scriptures concerning himself," for as they come to realize, their walking partner was Jesus himself. While this singular story may not be the model for every commute from Jerusalem to Emmaus, it does highlight the opportunity that our travels can provide to engage with Jesus.

## WHAT IS A LITURGY?

A liturgy is a pattern you systematically follow to offer worship to the Lord. Typically, a liturgy creates the structure for a corporate worship service and members of a church community experience this together. It can involve praising God for blessings, confessing sin, interceding for one another, offering resources back to God, asking for wisdom or help, and paying attention to what God is saying through Scripture or the Holy Spirit.

These same components of worship can provide structure to your commute, allowing you to orient your heart to God and be attentive to his direction throughout the day. The length and focus of your liturgy will depend on a number of things, including whether you are alone or with others and how long it takes you to get to work. But whether it is five minutes or fifty-five, using this time to worship God requires intentionality, practice, and a willingness to see time as a gift to be thoughtfully utilized.

There is no magic to the order of a liturgy; the pattern to it will not produce anything in and of itself. The specific practices in a liturgy do not transform us; rather, it is what God does through this time that changes us. A liturgy is simply a structured way of opening up ourselves to God's direction, reflecting on his power, authority, and goodness. It is worship. And in this worship we enter "the arena in which God recalibrates our hearts, reforms our desires, and rehabituates our loves. Worship isn't just something we do; it is where God does something to us. Worship is the heart of discipleship because it is the gymnasium in which God retrains our hearts."[2]

Just as having a morning workout routine can help wake up the body and build muscles in preparation for physical activities ahead, so a liturgy of commute opens the eyes of the soul and begins training our hearts in a trajectory toward God. By incorporating worship before we begin our work, our souls are aligned to hear from the Lord throughout the course of our day.

## Liturgy of Place

When you commute to work, you likely take a similar route each day. To implement a liturgy of commute, you can use the landmarks and cross streets of your route as a trigger for engaging with God. Praying for something specific at given cross streets, confessing as you drive by assigned landmarks, surrendering the workday to God at particular stoplights or freeway exits, and listening for what God might have you hear about your work and the people with whom you work, can make up the liturgy of your daily commute.

A daily liturgy of commute might also involve connecting the inner landscape of your heart with the outer physical landscape as you travel. Are there dark places in your heart? Then dark areas where you drive, walk, or bike might prompt you to reflect on what you may need to confess. Are there peaks or hills in your life or work for which you are grateful? Then when you crest a hill, thank God for them. What about the flat areas or long stretches that are relatively monotonous and unchanging? How might these areas prompt you to pray through the ordinariness of your work today? What other features of the landscape might provoke thoughtful reflection for you?

One friend's office is at the end of a long bridge. Each day as she commutes she uses the time driving over the bridge to remind herself of God's calling for her to be a bridge at work—a connection and conduit to share God's love with her colleagues. She found the experience to be particularly useful compared with other practices she had tried, because as she put it, "I was fresh and undistracted when I went over the bridge, so it was a great way to set up the day."

God can transform your commute—whether it is mundane or stressful, short or long—into an experience of worship and attentiveness to the Holy Spirit. You can be intentional about how you are shaped, and it begins with your commute. Even people who commute with others can participate in this practice. It may take some creativity, but it can be done. For instance, parents dropping their kids off at school can use this time to engage with them, discussing what they are thankful for, listening to a worship song, and praying for the day ahead out loud together. You could even do this if you are picking up other people's children by asking how you might pray for their day before you drop them off. If you carpool with coworkers, be intentional about listening to them. Ask about their concerns for the day, and if they are open to it, ask them how you might pray for them in the hours ahead. If you travel on public transportation, observe those around you and ask God to meet their needs.

If you travel to work alone, your commute may be the only time during the day when you have quiet and solitude. By entering into a liturgy of commute, you are being intentional about using this quiet time and space to begin the day "with" God as you travel to your place of work.

## *Liturgy and Attention*

Engaging in a liturgy of commute at the beginning of the day can turn our attention toward God and away from unhelpful distractions. You may have an important meeting scheduled or have residual emotions from the previous day's interactions with a coworker. You may be worried about something at home or just finished an intense phone conversation right before traveling to work. All of these things, along with the noise of traffic, can be distractions that keep your attention away from God. But God is there in the *midst of* the noise and emotions. By having a pattern of praying and worshipping, we can begin to train our hearts to be open to seeing things from God's perspective.

The garbage truck next to you may be God's way of speaking to you; and by intentionally being attentive to God's leading and guiding during your commute, you place yourself in the position of hearing from God. The conversation on the phone prior to leaving for work may be material for prayer during your liturgy. The train crossing that delays you may be God's way of providing more time for conversation with you. The liturgy provides the foundation for starting your day with God, offering yourself to be attentive to the Lord's voice, guidance, and direction. Beginning your workday intentionally conversing with God becomes a habit of your heart throughout the day.

Hearing from God at the beginning of your work may also change the trajectory of your work. You may hear something from him during your commute that you need to pay attention to at work. Without listening attentively to God on the way to work, you may not hear as clearly his instructions for the day. By paying attention to God's voice on the way in, we give ourselves to him in worship, surrendering to his agenda, and allowing our work to be for his sake, not our own.

## Liturgy and Surrender

The reality is that your commute will take you as long as it's going to take you on a given day. You may be able to control it a bit here and there by how fast you drive, run, or pedal; but for the most part, the length of your commute is beyond your control. This time can either be viewed as a curse or as a blessing—a gift for you given by God. As a gift, it can be a time to connect with God, enter into worship, and be reminded that life isn't about you but about the author of time. Tish Harrison Warren reflects on this concept:

> Time is a stream we are swept into. Time is a gift from God, a means of worship; . . . time is not a commodity that I control, manage or consume. The practice of liturgical time teaches me day by day, that time is not mine. It does not revolve around me. Time revolves around God—what he has done, what he is doing, and what he will do.[3]

By entering into our commute time with an intention to worship God, we acknowledge that we are not in charge of our time and instead seek to connect with the One who is in charge. Part of what can be so irritating about a commute is how much it reminds us that we are not in control. We cannot make the bus go faster, control the other drivers around us, or navigate our bikes faster than our bodies will go. This lack of control can certainly cause irritation; but by acknowledging God's presence in the midst of it, we can experience our mode of transportation as a gift and an opportunity to connect with him before we get to work.

We surrender our need for productivity at the beginning of the workday to God, who owns our time, skills, and resources. Before we begin our work, we surrender our desires to God, who is the master of our emotions and yearnings. We surrender our control over our days to God, who laid out each of our days prior to any of them coming to be. We surrender our plans, our vision, and our capacities to the originator of work itself, knowing that co-laboring with Christ is a delight and a privilege we should cherish.

A liturgy of commute can also be used on the way home from work. While at the beginning of the day, we may surrender our desires, our skills, and our control, at the end of the day we can surrender its events back to God. Did something go well at work? Praise him and express your gratitude for that. Did something agitate you at work today? Use your liturgy for paying attention to that event in his presence. Were you surprised by something that happened and were tempted to control it? Surrender the situation back to God. By expressing surrender both at the beginning and the end of the day, we place our control back into the hands of God, who has ultimate control over our lives and work in the first place.

## STORIES OF COMMUTE LITURGIES

### Aaron's Story

When Aaron—a writer, pastor, and liturgist—found himself in a particularly intense season at work, he became frustrated by his inability to reenter family life at the end of the workday. As the emotions, complexities, and stress from work began to spill over into his engagement with his wife and sons, he knew he had to find a remedy for this. He had a fifteen-minute commute to and from work, so he began considering how he might create something he could listen to each day that could help focus his mind and attention in a way that honored God, his work, and his family. He knew that the moment of crossing the threshold—into his work at the beginning of the day and returning to his family life at its end—was a particularly important time, and he wanted to be prepared for this transition each day.

Aaron gathered his musician friends, his writer friends, and his artist friends to collaborate on creating an audio recording for his travel time. Collaboratively, these friends came up with prayers, music, songs, and moments of silence, which they recorded for Aaron. This became the beginning of a project called "A New Liturgy"[4] where recordings of music, prayer, and Scripture of various lengths are combined to create a "sonic sanctuary" for different contexts. It is a beautiful example of redeeming a commute and inviting God's Spirit to usher in the workday. In Aaron's case, it also ended his workday, as he listened to the audio on his way home after work. The central theme of Aaron's recording was the Lord's Prayer. As he listened to it on the way to work and on the way home, it began to change his thinking and his emotional state. In the morning, instead of focusing on the intensity of the relationships he would encounter at work that day, he began focusing on the ways God was Lord in the midst of this intensity. Rather than be overwhelmed by what lay ahead, he found himself resting in the Lord, who would lead and guide his days and steps. And instead of coming home filled with the emotional strain of the day, he found he could enter into family life renewed by God's goodness and his provision. Using his commute time to engage with God enabled Aaron to surrender the outcomes of his work to God, as well as express gratitude after finishing the day's work.

## Elaine's Story

On most weekdays, Elaine walks from her house in a peaceful and still neighborhood to the school, where she drops her daughter off, and then on to her workplace at a private university. Elaine's job as a professor and researcher, however, is not peaceful and still. She is responsible to secure grants, teach, mentor, work on committees, write, and manage an academic program. In addition to her work, she has responsibilities as a spouse and parent, commitments to her church community, and she experiences the ordinary inundations of modern living. Elaine knows that peace and stillness are important and yet often elusive. During her walk to work she focuses on a three-part prayer to attune herself to God's peace.

After dropping her daughter off in the morning, Elaine spends the time between the school and the university praying a rendition of Psalm 46: "Let me be still and know that you are God." It is easy to be distracted by what was left undone at home, by what needs to be done in the hours ahead, by other thoughts that interrupt along the way. As the first part of her prayer, in response to these intruding thoughts, she repeats the phrase, "Let me be still . . ."

Once on campus, Elaine's walk takes her through a building-sized art installation, which has a square on top open to the sky. She uses this physical space as a reminder to reflect on God's love and presence. Here she shifts to the second part of her prayer: "Let me know that I am loved fully by God." In the academic culture, it is easy to want to impress so many others—colleagues, students, funders, reviewers, and so on. Elaine's prayer helps remind her that her worth is not dependent on her performance.

The last part of her walk takes her up several flights of stairs to her office. With each step, she repeats the third part of her prayer, "Let me enter into what you are doing today." Regardless of what the day holds, this prayer routine is a reminder that through her work she is participating in what God is already doing in the world.

## Will's Story

When Will worked as a director of a homeless shelter for men, he had a commute of about thirty minutes to and from work each day. Instead of using that commute to listen to the radio or music, Will enlisted the help of his pastor to help him redeem this time and craft a liturgy of commute, using landmarks as markers along the way. As he pulled out of his driveway and drove through his neighborhood, he focused on praying for his family and neighbors. Then as he turned into the city streets of his hometown, he prayed for the economic and spiritual flourishing of his city. Knowing the owners of several local shops helped enhance his intercession for those he knew in business there.

After driving through town, he then entered the freeway and drove several miles north to the shelter. The freeway gave Will a different view from the city, where he could see the mountains and the beauty of creation. This prompted him to begin thanking God for the beauty of creation and praising God for his character. At one point in his drive, the road passed the home of a young man from church whom Will was mentoring. This shifted his focus into a time of praying for the students of his church, their families, and their schools. Eventually, Will got off the freeway and drove a few minutes to the shelter. These few minutes gave Will an opportunity to pray for his work, the men he would come into contact with that day, and the various organizations that were partnering to provide support and care for the homeless.

This liturgy provided Will a time to prepare his heart and mind for the workday ahead. Coming into work after spending the thirty minutes in prayer helped Will connect with and hear from God about his work, his life, and his vocation as a church member. Since then, Will has moved to a different city. His commute has change from thirty minutes to about six minutes and he's no longer alone. On his way, he now drops off and picks up his son from school. Because Will has seen the power of the liturgy of commute, however, he has now been able to incorporate his son into this practice by saying out loud whatever they are grateful for on the way to school. Will's story is a reminder that these practices can be seasonal and may change over time. Whatever your commute or situation, these practices are meant to connect your everyday ordinary life and work with what God is doing in the world.

## THE PRACTICE OF A LITURGY OF COMMUTE

Think about your commute. You most likely go the same way every day or have a couple of routes you might use depending on traffic. Now think through the streets you take and the landmarks along the way. Do you pass a school, a particular store, or a certain street sign? Think about the topography of your commute. Do you see water, mountains, or farmland on your commute? Are there train tracks you cross or a hill you go up or down? Is there a particular house you pass that is interesting or unique?

Now begin mentally taking note of what you remember along the way on your commute. Use these landmarks as prompts to enter into different types of prayer for your commute. For instance, from your house to the first landmark, spend time praising God for the blessing of a new workday. After you cross the second landmark, move into a time of offering the day to the Lord. At landmark three, you may begin asking for God's help in your work; and then after passing landmark four, begin praying for others in your life who need it. After passing the last landmark on your commute, use the rest of the time to ask God what he desires you to be attentive to at work that day.

Perhaps part of your commute is spent on public transportation and the noise of your surroundings makes it difficult for you to sustain attention on interacting with God. In this situation, you might use the time to read or listen to Scripture or a podcast (with headphones of course!). Perhaps you can listen to music that focuses your time and attention on God's goodness and purposes. One of the tools we have found quite valuable for ourselves is "Pray as You Go,"[5] a daily ten- to fifteen-minute podcast devotional that includes music, a Scripture reading, and a time of reflection.

How you craft your own liturgy of commute is up to you, but you may want to start with identifying the components of worship in which you want to engage: praising God, confessing sin, thanking God for his blessings, listening to Scripture, reflecting on the attributes of God, interceding for others, requesting God's direction and guidance, and so on. Then consider the landmarks you encounter on your commute and connect each one to a different aspect of your desired liturgy. This will help your mind not to wander as you travel.

After a time, you may have the liturgy memorized, but at the beginning you may want to write down your intentions to help you remember it. Creating a new habit while commuting may seem clunky at first, but stick with it. Be creative about it. Experiment with it. If something isn't working, change it. Find what works for you in this liturgy, so that your commute can be a tool God uses to transform you in your work. Remember, this is something you are practicing, not something to be perfected. This liturgy is about relationship with God, and you can view your commute as a tool to prompt an experience of conversation with the Lord.

One way to create a liturgy of commute is to write down a list of things you want to surrender to God, people for whom you want to pray, and things for which you want to thank God. Take this list with you and start going through it as you pass your commute's landmarks. Over time, engaging in this practice consistently will direct your mind, heart, and body toward a posture of worship, surrender, and attention on your drive, ride, or walk.

## QUESTIONS FOR REFLECTION OR DISCUSSION

After you have practiced your liturgy of commute for a week or two, reflect on the following questions, either by yourself or in a small group:

1. *What was important for you to include in your liturgy? Why?*

2. *How did you craft your liturgy? Was it around landmarks, the landscape, or something else?*

3. *What have you experienced as you've engaged in this liturgy of commute?*

4. *How has God shaped you, spoken to you, or transformed your work through this practice?*

5. *What would you like to incorporate into your liturgy as you go forward? What might be helpful for you to leave behind?*

## 2

# WORKPLACE AS HOLY GROUND

## THE HOLY ORDINARY

For each of us, our office space is quite ordinary. Even the most gorgeous corner office with a view can lose its luster when the grind of ordinary work is conducted within its four walls. In all the ordinariness of our work and our office spaces, it can be easy to forget that to God, space and place matter—and they matter a whole lot.

As we read Scripture, we see repeatedly that God uses space and place to speak, to transform people, and to further his work. But many times, we gloss over this. We also forget the ordinariness of the examples of work in the Scriptures. We see heroes of the faith—elevating them and their vocations—forgetting that at the point where God intervenes, they are just going about their ordinary, everyday lives.

Take the story of Moses and the burning bush as an example (see Exod. 3:1–12). Most of us see this story as extraordinary; we were introduced to it as a miraculous story of God's encounter with Moses and ultimately the Hebrew people. And it is. But it is also filled with the normal, the everyday, the mundane. Try stepping back from the story as you've always read it and put yourself in Moses' shoes. He had once been a prince in an Egyptian palace. He knew extravagance, he knew power, he knew the extraordinary. But here in the book of Exodus, we see him in a different light. He's not in a palace surrounded by luxury, but rather in the middle of the wilderness watching after a bunch of his father-in-law's sheep. It is in this very ordinary—and maybe even desolate—workplace setting that God makes himself known to Moses through the burning bush.

Talk about ordinary. The wilderness, the desert, a stark land of solitude. Moses is by himself with a flock of smelly, needy, stubborn sheep. When you read this story through the lens of work, you see that even Moses had a truly ordinary job to do. His job was to keep track of the sheep, to find them pasture, and to move them to where they could graze or find water. Although this was a deeply important job in rural cultures, nevertheless it was quite ordinary.

It is into this ordinariness that God speaks. Moses is in his office—his mountainside office—going about his everyday work, probably not expecting to hear from, commune with, or worship God.

But isn't that how the Spirit of God works? It is into these earthy ordinary elements that God chooses to speak. God doesn't take Moses aside to a place where he would pay attention; God's Spirit enters the very space where Moses *already is.*

Think about that for a moment. Moses—liberator of the people of Israel, the man God uses to lead his people for decades—doesn't have to be brought away from his actual life to hear from God. It's *in the midst* of his ordinary life that God enters, speaks, and is worshipped. God shows up in a bush on fire, and then he sets apart Moses' mountain office and consecrates it as holy ground. He takes the ordinary elements of dirt, rocks, plants, and fire, and he separates them as elements of communion and connection. He marks them as a place where Moses heard from the Lord himself.

God tells Moses to take his sandals off, because God names the ordinariness of the mountain and the bush as holy ground. Of course, the ground is holy because God is present. But the truth is that God is *always* present. God was present to Moses in that moment of calling, and God is present to us in our own ordinary workplaces.

We elevate this story as grand and as a pivotal point in the story of the Lord's people. Certainly, this is true. But it is not what Moses had expected for his workday, and it's certainly not how most of us enter our workdays. We believe that God wants that to change for you. God longs for Christian workers to anticipate God showing up and speaking into the midst of our work.

What if you started to see your work, your ordinary everyday work, as God saw Moses' work: As a space where God wants to speak and commune with you and, in turn, be worshipped by you? What might change if you started expecting God to show up in your office or workplace in all its ordinariness?

## BLESSING OF PLACE

Throughout Scripture, we see examples of God marking the ordinary as holy and the blessings that emerge when people recognize the holiness in the ordinary. One of the most salient examples of this occurred when Jesus took the mundane elements of bread and wine, blessed them, and used them as an object lesson for his disciples at his last Passover on earth. When we practice communion, the everyday bread and wine remind us of Jesus' sacrifice and God's love for us; and this practice also reminds us that we ourselves—as flawed and human as we are—are also holy and set apart for God's purposes (see 1 Pet. 1:15–16).

In the Old Testament, God provided guidance to the Hebrew people so they could recognize holiness in the ordinary—and this guidance was specific and location based. When they were entering the Promised Land, the injunction to remember God's commands was front and center. The people of God were to talk about his commands, share them with their children, and write them on the doorframes of their houses and gates. Marking the house in this way was a reminder that this home—where the family gathered, where meals were eaten, and often where one's work was done—

was no longer ordinary, but rather a place in which God could be encountered.

From ancient times until today, practicing Jews affix to their front doorframe a *mezuzah*—a small case holding a piece of parchment inscribed with the *Shema* prayer, which begins, "Hear O Israel: The LORD our God, the LORD is one" (Deut. 6:4–9). The *mezuzah* is a way of reminding those in the house not only of God's commands but also that the house they are about to enter is a place set aside as holy to God.[1] A blessing is said when putting up the *mezuzah*, and those entering and leaving the house will often touch it as a reminder of the blessing. And so the *mezuzah* is a tangible way of symbolizing that both the house and the daily activities of its inhabitants—while appearing mundane—have been marked as holy and set aside for God's purposes. The ordinary has become extraordinary through God's presence.

The idea of a dwelling place made holy appears over and over throughout Scripture. In each instance, we see an ordinary place become holy when God enters in. Moses refers to the burning bush as a place where God dwelled (see Deut. 33:16). When the Hebrew people wandered in the wilderness, the portable tabernacle was God's dwelling place. The notion of God dwelling in the ordinary is seen most significantly when in the person of Jesus God becomes flesh and dwells among us (see John 1:14). And New Testament passages even refer to Christ dwelling in us (see Eph. 3:16–17a)! A dwelling has a humble connotation. It is a place where people work, play, and sleep. It is where daily life happens. When God shows up, the ordinary becomes holy. And we know that God always shows up.

In a similar way, when you recognize that the place where you work is holy ground, you can invoke God's blessing in that space and wherever your organization's work is done. Walking the hallways in prayer, saying a blessing over the office doors in your building, praying for the meeting rooms, the cafeteria, the production spaces within your workplace, the routes where the company cars drive, and asking God's blessing over what happens there—these are all ways of recognizing your workplace as holy ground. And this recognition cannot help but change us and the ways in which we interact with our work and with our coworkers.

## WORKPLACE AS HOLY GROUND

God desires to be deeply involved in the work you are doing, whether technical or creative, with numbers or paint, with people or chemicals, with nature or law enforcement, with selling something or creating something. God is in your ordinary work and workplace, whatever that space is for you.

You may not work in an office. Your workplace may be a home where you care for young children, an elderly person, or someone sick. Your workplace may be your vehicle, as you travel for work or transport goods. Your workplace may be a kitchen where you cook or bake, the hallways of a school where you teach or clean, a playing field where you coach, or a barn where you take care of animals.

Workplace is not limited and the good news is that neither is God! Wherever you work, whatever that space is, it can be a place of connection and communion in your relationship with Christ. If your workplace can be a sanctuary of worship, as we saw in the story of Moses, then the place where you go about your work is *holy ground.*

Think about your workplace for a minute. Is it a cubicle or a medical office? Is it a dentist's chair or a classroom? Is it outside or in a factory? Is it a corner office, behind a register, or in a large shared room? Whatever that physical space is for you, it is a place that can be seen as holy ground because God has already set it apart—just as he set apart the ground where Moses worked. It is a place where God can speak to you and be with you, and where you can respond in worship to God *through* your work.

## STORIES OF HOLY GROUND

### *Kristie's Story*

When we orient to our workplace as holy ground, we begin to see our work differently. Kristie is someone who gets this deeply. Kristie is a performing artist and a mathematician. An unusual, but wonderful combination. For several years, Kristie was a high school drama and math teacher. But through a series of circumstances, she went to work in accounts payable at a technology firm.

Kristie's job was to send invoices out to the company's clients and pay the company's bills. All . . . day . . . long. It was an ordinary job. Still, it was an ordinary job that was also deeply important—not only to the company but, as Kristie came to see, to God as well.

She didn't work in a plush office space. She worked in a small cubicle. But as she began to learn and think about worshipping God through her work, something began to change in her. If work could be worship, then her cubicle was the temple where she offered her worship to the Lord. Doing her best work would be a way in which she would honor God at work.

After having thought through this idea, she came to her church's work discipleship group very excited. She began to talk about her cubicle as holy ground, and how this perspective had changed everything for her. As a result, her work was invigorated in a new way. As she was paying bills and sending out invoices, she became aware of how this work was contributing both to her own organization and to those in other companies. She recognized that working diligently was an important way to commune with God and to hear from him. The ordinariness of it all wasn't lost on Kristie, because she had come to know God, as Moses did, as the God who enters the ordinary to speak to and be with his people.

Then Kristie took it one step further: She began to think about the others who stepped into that sacred space. If her cubicle was holy ground, then it wasn't just holy ground for her. It was holy ground for anyone who stepped into that space, whether they knew it or not.

"This will change how I respond to interruptions from coworkers or from my boss when I'm already very busy," she said. Rather than being frustrated with the interruptions, Kristie began to view them as opportunities God was bringing to her, which enabled her to give her whole attention to the person who had entered the holy ground of her cubicle.

Seeing her literal office space as holy ground changed Kristie. It changed how she thought about her work and how she engaged in it. It changed the ways she experienced God at work. And it changed how she thought about and interacted with others in her little corner of the company where she worked.

## Matt's Story

Matt is another Christian who has seen God consecrate the space in which he works. Matt is a visual artist. He combines the regular practice of walking around Seattle with his artistic talent to create beautifully complex drawings and paintings of his routes. As he walks, he prays for the places and spaces he passes through, contemplating his relationship to the earth and to the urban jungle in which he lives.

Through these walks, Matt has developed a deep theology of place that he has taken to the educational institutions where he is on faculty. One particular setting in which he has experienced God deeply is a dingy stairway at the technical college where he teaches computer classes. Every morning, Matt ascends the stairs to the computer lab where he meets his students. And in this stairway, he prays. As a result, this stairway has become a profound place of holy ground for him. He shared the following, along with a picture of this stairwell in a social media post:

Looking out the window from the stairwell of [my college], where in the mornings I teach computer tech classes. I pray in this stairwell every morning. It is my chapel. I pray for my students, who come from all walks of life, mostly marginalized, immigrants, African Americans, Latinos, some who struggle with learning disabilities. I pray that I would serve them well, equip them with good knowledge, love them.

Though in the distance things are dim, unclear, this morning I again stand in the stairwell. This morning I have work to do—the same work I've been doing—trying to be of service, create opportunities for all, loving others. This school is small, underfunded, unglamorous, and sometimes heartbreaking. But this morning I am here, I recommit to this work, and the enemies of our work will have to shut us down or throw me out to stop me, and even then I will find another way to keep going and doing the work of today.

## Jeff's Story

There are some specific ways we can remind ourselves that our workplaces are opportunities for encountering the holy in the ordinary. Just as Jews use a *mezuzah* as a reminder of God's presence, we can use everyday items or experiences in the workplace to remind us that God is here with us in the midst of the ordinary and that he wants to engage with us in our work.

Jeff works as a contract consultant for a tech firm. When he began to consider the idea that his workplace was holy ground where he might encounter God, he decided to acknowledge God's presence and pray a blessing over his workplace as he entered the building each day. Like many employees in the tech industry, he uses a key card to get into the buildings. The activity of swiping his key card to enter became a prompt for Jeff to ask God to bless the place. Every time he came in to work, returned from lunch, or moved from one building to another, Jeff was reminded that God was with him in this ordinary office building, and so he would ask God to bless his workplace.

## YOUR WORKPLACE—IT'S HOLY GROUND TOO!

Different people. Different stories. Different calls from God to see the space and place of work as set apart for God's purposes. Each story is a reminder that we too can be people committed to seeing God in the ordinary. Each of us can be used by God to bless our place of work. When we see our workplaces as holy ground, it reorients our understanding of work to better align with God's. It may change the way we actually do our work or engage with others.

You may read these stories and feel inspired. If that is the case, we hope they will encourage you to connect with God in all of the places he has deemed as holy. You may also read these stories and feel discouraged—sensing that your workplace and your work are too ordinary, too mundane for God to inhabit. Maybe you have gotten lost in the monotony your work and find it hard to believe that God could breathe new life into the space where you go about your everyday tasks.

If that is you, please hear this.

You do not need an extraordinary job or life or workspace to connect with and be used by God. God has always used the ordinary to accomplish his purposes: an unwed teenager in Roman controlled Palestine, bread and wine as sacraments, and ordinary Christians throughout the world going about their daily work. When God indwells ordinary things, they become extraordinary— the holy ordinary. God can use dingy staircases, cubicles, and mountainsides just as well as the corner office with a view. Your work does not have to be glamorous or newsworthy to be used in God's kingdom; he is just as pleased with the work of the custodian as that of the CEO. If that work is done with an attitude of worship and expectancy, then God will reveal himself.

It is not the spectacular that God generally uses, but the everyday. What makes our work most extraordinary has nothing to do with us and everything to do with God showing up in the midst of the mundane and bringing a new perspective. A miracle indeed!

What would it look like for you to think about your workplace as holy ground? What would change for you if you started each day giving your workspace back to the Lord, set apart as holy?

## THE PRACTICE OF WORKPLACE AS HOLY GROUND

When God spoke to Moses in his workplace at Mount Horeb, he had him take off his shoes as a symbol of consecration, of setting apart and giving back to the Lord the space in which he stood. The practice of workplace as holy ground involves just that—a setting apart and a remembrance of God's consecration. As we have seen, it might be a prayer in a stairwell or a blessing as you swipe your card key. It may be experiencing God while sending invoices or praying that God's purposes would be accomplished in your company's conference rooms. What might it look like in your workplace?

Try devoting two weeks (ten working days) to this practice. Repetition involving your regular work rhythms will help this practice be meaningful and transformative. As you enter your workplace at the beginning of the day, do so at a slower pace than normal. Maybe you ride an elevator to get to your floor, regularly walk through the same hallway to get your cubicle, or hold a key to get into your office. Use these physical objects or spaces as a reminder to you to participate in this practice. Maybe there's a threshold in a doorway that you enter. Maybe it's a gate to a field or a door to a car.

As you are riding the elevator, or walking that hallway, or unlocking your door, use this time to breathe a prayer of consecration. For example, you could say something like:

> *God, since my work is an act through which you can be worshipped, then the place in which I go about my work matters to you. I choose today to set this space apart to you, the physical setting in which I go about my work. This place is holy ground, set apart for your glory and for the furtherance of the kingdom. May I hear from you today in this place.*

Then, as you go about your day, choose something in your regular rhythm of work that will serve as a prompt to remind you. This could be something that happens at the same time every day or a reminder on your phone or computer set to go off at a certain time. Whatever it is, find a way to remind yourself of your holy ground perspective and practices for that day.

We encourage you to keep track of how this practice is going throughout the two-week period and then reflect on your experiences.

## QUESTIONS FOR REFLECTION OR DISCUSSION

1. *How is the practice of setting apart your workspace going? Do you find it easy or difficult to incorporate this into your workday? Why? How are you reminding yourself that your workplace is holy ground?*

2. *What difference does viewing your workplace as holy ground make in how you think about and engage in the work that you do? How does it impact your interactions with coworkers or customers, your boss or vendors?*

3. *Is setting a reminder for this practice going well? Is your reminder working? Why or why not? If not, what could you change to make it more effective?*

4. *What are you hoping God will do in your workspace over the next two weeks?*

# 3

# SURRENDERING THE CALENDAR

The problem with work is that we always have more, right? The to-do lists are a mile long, and the clock has only so many hours. You might have a seemingly productive few hours checking things off your list, only to go to a meeting and be assigned another project, with another to-do list a mile long. Or you might block off time to get the nagging to-do list dwindled down, only to open your e-mail and discover that you have three urgent things to handle before day's end! The work cultures of many companies and organizations promote this type of never-ending urgency and demand for results.

We go to sleep thinking about all the things we need to do the next day, and we work to try to beat the clock so we can get the most done in the shortest amount of time. Many employers have come up with ways to reward those who are the most productive—those making the biggest sales, manufacturing the largest number of products, carrying the heaviest loads, serving the most customers, reaching the widest audience, or having students who get the highest test scores.

This working environment has proved destructive for many, causing burn out, depression, and weariness in our souls. Many people suffer from anxiety, stress disorders, and a general sense that life is a treadmill—always on and always moving. We fear that if we slow down even the slightest bit, we will turn into those cartoon characters who fall off the treadmill and bounce and bounce . . . and finally stop moving. Quantifying work has seeped into our daily routines, and in many cases has caused more harm than good.

While working hard may be positive, constantly being hurried and having the pressure to perform at a frantic pace is not.

## THE DIFFERENCE BETWEEN BUSY AND HURRIED

Busy is not inherently bad. When we look at the Gospels, Jesus' ministry was busy: It was filled with people, projects (a big kingdom building project, if you remember), travels, and teachings. Jesus would leave one region only to find multitudes of people waiting for him at the next. In the course of days, he preached and taught thousands—*and* fed them, healed them, and instructed them to spread the good news. While Jesus was busy, however, he was never hurried. John Ortberg makes this helpful distinction in his book *Soul Keeping*:

> Being busy is an outward condition, a condition of the body. It occurs when we have many things to do. . . . There are limits to how much busy-ness we can tolerate . . . [but] by itself, busy-ness is not lethal. . . . Being hurried is an inner condition, a condition of the soul. It means to be so preoccupied with myself and my life that I am unable to be fully present with God, with myself and with other people. I am unable to occupy this present moment. Busy-ness migrates to hurry when we let it squeeze God out of our lives. I cannot live in the kingdom of God with a hurried soul. I cannot rest in God with a hurried soul.[1]

Maybe that is the difference between how we operate and how Jesus operated. The pace he kept and those interactions with that number of people could easily have caused Jesus to have a hurried heart, a hurried body, a hurried soul. But he never appeared hurried in the Gospels. Instead, we find Jesus deeply present with those with him. To those who had searched for him, he revealed himself. He did not consider them as interruptions; rather, he recognized people as important and fully attended to each one in the present moment.

We may think Jesus could do this because he was fully God. He had the supernatural power to accomplish great things in a short amount of time. But in this we forget that he was also fully human. His productivity had nothing to do with his divine nature. In fact, for Jesus, as Emily P. Freeman says, "'staying productive' meant abiding in His Father no matter what."[2]

The number of activities that filled Jesus' calendar did not seem to change the ways he went about his work. The main factor, consistent across all of his to-do lists and appointments, was his ability to stay, to remain, to live in the presence of his Father in the midst of his work. He was not concerned with how much he could get done; but rather he was keenly aware that to accomplish the call of God on his life, he would need to be laser-focused on the tasks God the Father had given to him *in each moment*. This enabled him to live deeply connected to God and also deeply present with those to whom God had called him. Jesus knew the power of living life wide open before God. The apostle Paul picks up on Jesus' ability to live both deeply connected to God and deeply connected to people, and he instructs followers of Jesus to do the same.

## YOUR LIFE AS AN OFFERING

In the book of Romans, Paul exhorts believers not to live according to the culture around them—always hurried, frantically striving for that which could never satisfy. He gives them a warning but then offers them a solution and an alternative way to live:

> So here's what I want you to do, God helping you: Take your everyday, ordinary life—your sleeping, eating, going-to-work, and walking-around life—and place it before God as an offering. Embracing what God does for you is the best thing you can do for him. Don't become so well-adjusted to your culture that you fit into it without even thinking. Instead, fix your attention on God. You'll be changed from the inside out. Readily recognize what he wants from you, and quickly respond

to it. Unlike the culture around you, always dragging you down to its level of immaturity, God brings the best out of you, develops well-formed maturity in you. (Rom. 12:1–2 The Message)

Other translations instruct the believer "to offer your bodies as a living sacrifice" (NIV) or to "present your bodies as a living and holy sacrifice" (NASB).

Here is the reality: Our calendars and to-do lists, obligations and desires dictate what our bodies do, where they go, and how we use them. Many of the items on our calendars have to do with commitments, requirements, responsibilities for work, and tasks assigned to us.

In some seasons and in some jobs, we might have more autonomy over how our time is used, and we are able to decide the details of our work: with whom we will meet and when, what tasks we will allocate our time to do, and what projects we plan to accomplish. Alternatively, we may be at the mercy of others who decide what we should be doing and when. Either way, however, as our calendars fill up and as our to-do lists grow, these activities and tasks provide a framework for how we might give ourselves to God.

Paul's words in Romans 12 are in stark contrast to those cultural values that promote hustle, hurry, activity, and achievement. Instead, Paul promotes a completely different way of living. This is the way of sacrifice, where we take our desires and obligations, our daily tasks and our long-term responsibilities, and we offer them to God. An offering is something freely given, something voluntarily given up for someone else's sake. What Paul is calling us to is completely different from the work culture in which many of us find ourselves. Yes, God wants you to work with excellence, to do all you can to do the job well—whether you are cleaning toilets or selling hedge funds. That is not in question here. What Paul is getting at is our motivations.

Are you working to achieve the next goal, to make the highest numbers, or to reach the next level on the ladder? Are you working to please a boss or someone else whose opinion matters in your life? Are you working to provide a better life for your children or for yourself? Or are you instead working to be a living offering to the Lord? Your desires, responsibilities, and even obligations may not be bad in and of themselves; but if our first priority is not offering ourselves to God and pleasing him, then we will quickly find ourselves desiring the wrong thing, working for ourselves and being pulled away from focusing on what God wants for our work.

We must become aware of the motivations of our hearts in order to realign them toward focusing on what God wants for our work. The problem, though, is that many of us do not know for what or whom we are working. We have a hard time always knowing why we do what we do. Our hearts have blind spots, making it hard to see our way back to the ways of working as a living offering. If you take a look at your calendar and your to-do lists, then you will see how your obligations and desires affect your work.

## AN EXPERIMENT IN DESIRE AND OBLIGATION

Try a little experiment: Pull out your calendar and your to-do list. It may be on your phone, on your computer, or in a planner, but find wherever it is you keep your lists and flip them open. Now, pause after reading this paragraph and scan your lists for what is happening this week. As you scan, notice how many of the items are things you are obligated to do as opposed to things that you have the freedom to engage in or not. Next, identify whether the things you are obligated to do are things you enjoy and would do even if they were not required. Are these obligations desirable to you? Or are they tasks that must be accomplished or meetings you must attend, but that you would just as soon avoid if you could?

At this point, you should have mentally organized your to-do list into three categories:

1. *Desirable Obligations—Anything required by your work or your role that you also look forward to and enjoy.*

2. *Desirable Options—Those engagements or tasks not required by your work, but which you have chosen to pursue because you enjoy them.*

3. *Undesirable Obligations—Those activities, meetings, or responsibilities that you don't enjoy, but that you must do as a part of your job.*

Go ahead and write down your tasks in three columns, corresponding to these three categories.

You can use the table at the end of this chapter if you like. For now, put the list aside, and we will revisit it at the end of the chapter.

Let's go back to the verses in Romans 12. Paul says we should place our lives, our working lives, before God as offerings. This command *to place* or *offer* or *present* has the connotation of willingly giving God your life and all that it entails. Holding tight to your schedule and struggling through your to-do list is completely opposite from what Paul says God desires from us.

Surrender and sacrifice your desires—this is what God wants from you. This is the first step, the giving up to God. But we don't just give ourselves up to God. In this process, God re-creates us and fills our minds with new things. God gives us the mind of Christ so that we begin to desire what the Lord wants, and we begin to see better the things God wants us to do. In a sense, when we offer ourselves to God, we are then given new things to do during our days. Or we may be given new ways of doing the things to which God was already calling us.

To-do lists are not wrong. God does not hate your calendar, and your schedule is not necessarily in opposition to God's purposes. Indeed, your to-do list and calendar can be tools through which the Lord guides your motivations, directs your obligations, and gives you the grace to be a living sacrifice. God's agenda for your day might even be accomplished *through* the items on your calendar! But by offering your calendar—your desirable obligations, your desirable options, and your undesirable obligations—up to God, you allow the Lord to speak into your activities. When you surrender your calendar, you open up yourself to letting go of your expectations for the day and allowing your schedule to be shaped by God's intentions for your work. Does this mean that the Lord may be asking you not to follow through on your commitments? Most likely not. But your loving heavenly Father may be asking you to approach a task, project, conversation, or interaction differently than you would have if you did not carry it out with the desire to be a living sacrifice for God's purposes.

## OFFERING YOUR CALENDAR

So, how do we do this? How can we practice on a regular basis what Paul exhorts us to do in Romans 12? This is where the practice of surrendering the calendar comes in. In this practice, you hold your to-do lists lightly and ask what God would have for you today. What might God want you to have on your calendar? How does God want you to interact with those around you? As you hear the voice of the Savior, you can begin to surrender to God's agenda. One way this can be done is by praying through a to-do list before you start your work. You can also pull out your calendar at the beginning of the day and pray through your appointments, asking God to speak to you about them. You could do this on a weekly basis, as you sit down to prepare for the week ahead. By paying attention to God's agenda for the day, or week, you begin to let go of your own.

You can practice this at the start of your day or immediately before beginning any task or appointment. You could even revisit this practice on a break, reminding yourself of what God impressed upon you previously. This may be extremely difficult at first, especially if you are used to allowing other motivations to determine how you spend your time. But be encouraged! The second part of Romans 12 holds a promise: "You'll be changed from the inside out" (Rom. 12:2 The Message). Another translation says it this way: "God will transform you into a new person by changing the way you think" (Rom. 12:2 NLT).

By surrendering your calendar and to-do list to God each day, you allow God to change the way you think about your work, change your motivations for work, and eventually change the way you structure your work, including what you put on your to-do list and your calendar- transforming who you are in the process.

## SMALL TWEAKS, BIG IMPACT

At the heart of this practice is actively seeking out and listening to the voice of God. By giving God's voice priority, you begin to set a precedent for giving him what truly belongs to the Lord anyway: your work, your tasks, your very life.

As you engage in this practice, your tasks for the day might stay the same, but the Lord may prompt you to make a small tweak as to how you are to accomplish a certain task. For instance, you may hear God tell you to ask a coworker for input into a project or conversation that day. Perhaps this task could have been accomplished on your own; but by asking for input, you put yourself in a humble position to listen carefully to your colleague. You may hear that God wants you to serve others in each interaction you have, or you may hear God tell you to interact with your boss and coworkers in a different way.

When you engage in the practice of surrendering the calendar, you may find that instead of prioritizing productivity and crossing off tasks, God wants you to spend time with a coworker who is hurting and needs a loving person to be present with them. This may throw off what *you* had in mind for your day, but that is the way of loving sacrifice. We set down our desires and trade them for the Savior's desires.

You may find that you do not want to do a number of the tasks on your calendar or to-do list. These tasks are among your undesirable obligations. Many of us take jobs because we need the money, and therefore the work itself may not have any intrinsic meaning to us, or perhaps it alienates us from what we find really important in the world. We may feel that our work does not provide us with opportunities for personal development or advancement, or maybe it is just flat out boring. Or perhaps we feel caught between the demands of our jobs and the demands of other aspects of our lives— maybe you have a desire to be home more with your family, or to do volunteer work, but you cannot afford to work fewer hours.[3]

Giving performance reviews, restocking a warehouse, transporting goods long distances, cleaning up after children, or working with a difficult person can all be tasks that we experience as drudgery. Just because they are undesirable, however, does not necessarily mean that we should not do them. Often, it is through these undesirable obligations that God transforms us.

If your job is highly dictated by a boss or by the nature of the work itself, you can still participate in this spiritual practice of laying your to-do list and calendar before God, allowing the Giver of your work the opportunity to speak into your day. God may not change your to-do list, but he may change the attitude with which your work is accomplished. By listening to God's voice as you review your daily tasks, you are training yourself to give him authority over your work.

This way of working and living, though, can be risky. Listening to God's voice can create all sorts of interruptions in our lives. But isn't that the point of this practice? When we do our work as living sacrifices, we begin to engage in life as people who see our lives as *Christ's* life lived through us, for the glory of God.

## STORIES OF SURRENDERING THE CALENDAR

### Shannon's Story

A while ago, I (Shannon) was having a hard time holding all the details of my work in my head. I felt that there was too much to do and too little time to accomplish it all. This feeling of being overwhelmed led to the fear that I was going to forget something

I needed to do. At the time, I was in charge of running events for a faith and work program at a seminary, and these events often involved lots of small details. I didn't know when I would forget an important detail, but I knew I couldn't keep everything straight.

I had two problems. First, I had too much to do; my list was virtually impossible to tackle in the amount of time I had. My second problem was that all of my to-dos were just that: *my* to-dos, *my* agenda, *my* priorities. These were the things *I* was putting pressure on myself to get done. Sure, many of them needed to be done in order to serve those I was assisting in the program, but the pressure I was putting on myself was not placed there by anyone else. These were *my* agendas. Not necessarily God's.

So, out of desperation and driven by the fear of dropping one of the balls I was juggling, I prayed. I told the Lord I couldn't hold everything straight and lamented that there were too many pieces to my work. I gave my to-do list back to God, trusting that the Lord could hold it all. I then asked to be filled with the Lord's agenda. I surrendered my calendar and to-do list back to God, knowing that if I couldn't make it all work together, certainly Christ could.

While participating in this practice didn't make my to-do list shorter, I was prompted by the Holy Spirit to do things to which I don't think I would have paid attention had I not given my calendar and my to-do list over to the Lord.

By surrendering my agenda and listening for God's voice, I remembered a critical detail about an upcoming event that hadn't crossed my mind during the previous week. This was a detail that had I forgotten it would have caused me much more work to fix after the deadline had passed. The Holy Spirit's enabling my mind to remember this detail was a sheer gift of grace.

Then two college girls sat down next to me at the coffee shop where I was working. One was studying theology and the other geology. I could have been easily annoyed by their distracting conversation, because of the amount of work I needed to get done. But, instead of being distracted by their conversation, I was prompted to pray for them and their future work, that they would hear the call of God and work for his glory. These things weren't on my to-do list for the day. Pausing to pray. Being reminded about an important detail. But, amazingly, when I gave into the Holy Spirit's promptings and lived in God's agenda, I was able to get my list done.

This practice has helped me see that Jesus was on to something with his constant awareness of being in the presence of the Father. It wasn't just because Jesus was God that he was able to accomplish so much during his earthly ministry (remember, he was fully human too!). It was because he worked in the power of the Father's presence that Jesus was able to engage in his ministry without hurry, without frantic stress, and with the love of God backing him. Because I gave the Lord's voice precedence over my desire for productivity, God revealed that being Lord over time, the Holy Spirit can also work *through* us to accomplish the tasks that are desirable obligations, undesirable obligations, and even those things we desire to do by choice.

### Dan's Story

Dan is a project manager at a major tech company, managing a team of over two hundred people who work on three continents. To say his to-do lists are long and his calendar is full is an understatement. But Dan is keenly aware of the difference it makes when he gives God his agenda at work. So, most days he begins his work, not by opening his computer to answer e-mails, but by reading Scripture at his desk and then asking God for *his* agenda for Dan's meetings, who he needs to pay attention to most on his team, and how he can work for God's glory, not his own. Dan pulls out his to-do list and his calendar on his phone and literally prays through each task and each meeting before his day begins.

Dan's work has been transformed because he has been transformed through this practice. He now views his work as an opportunity to connect with God in each meeting, while he is working on each project and during his interactions with each person on his team. Even in the midst of the pressure to perform at a high level, Dan's practice of surrendering his calendar has shaped his priorities to be centered on being a vessel of God's love and hope in a highly competitive work environment. The practice of surrendering the calendar has been a catalyst for giving God priority in his work and attuning himself to hear from God throughout the day. By paying attention to the Holy Spirit's prompting on his to-do lists and tasks, Dan can work with excellence, love, and care in some profound ways.

## THE PRACTICE OF SURRENDERING THE CALENDAR

Consider how you can pay attention to God in new ways by surrendering your to-do list, asking for God's help, and listening for what he would have you do each day at work. How can you go about using this practice in your daily work? As you begin this practice, take a few minutes thinking about the following questions:

1. *What does God have to say about the current pace of your work culture? Remember that busy is not necessarily bad, but are you living hurried?*


2. *What can you do to align yourself with God's pace and God's agenda for your work? What might that pace and agenda be?*


After thinking about these questions, write down your impressions and responses as this will be helpful as you start this practice.

Begin this practice of surrendering the calendar by intentionally setting a time to go over your schedule or your to-do list. You may have a regular time in your work rhythm when you already do this. If so, then incorporate the practice of surrendering your calendar into this set time. It may be on a Sunday before your work week begins, it may be the beginning of each day, or the first day of the month. This time might be every Friday before you go home for the weekend. *When* you go over your calendar and to-do list does not matter; what matters is that you regularly incorporate this practice.

Now plan to add an extra ten minutes or longer to this time. Listening takes time and practice. You might not hear from God about your calendar in the split second you inquire about it; in fact, you probably won't. In this case, set aside some time to prayerfully reflect on your upcoming schedule.

As you pull up your calendar, take a few minutes to breathe deeply. Often looking through what we have to do can bring up anxiety and trigger stress hormones in our bodies. Invite God to be in your planning and ask him how to respond to the stress when it surfaces. Pray that you might hear what God has to say about your agenda. One by one, go through each day (or each task) and read through it slowly. As you read, pause and ask God if there is anything you need to hear about that day or task. It may be helpful to write down what you hear—you could even do this as a comment next to the task or as a note on the meeting reminder.

As you listen, take a posture of surrender. Give the day, the meeting, or task over to God. Remember that you can't control what you hear; but if you put yourself into a posture of listening, this will allow the Lord's voice to be louder than the other voices vying for your attention—your boss's approval, your own sense of productivity, or the motivations that hinder you from surrendering to God. It may be helpful to hold your body in a position of surrender and openness—perhaps by opening your hands to show a willingness to let go of your own agenda, and a desire to receive insight and wisdom from God.

Now, look back over the motivations list you made with your tasks and appointments in three categories. Which are the Desirable Obligations—things you are obligated to do that you also enjoy?

Thank God for these tasks and interactions. Are there ways in which you can see God using these things to further kingdom purposes?

Which items are Desirable Options—things you do not have to do but you enjoy and are fulfilled by? How can you honor God with your desires toward these tasks or meetings?

Which items are Undesirable Obligations—tasks or interactions that may be difficult or do not bring you joy? Can God bring new life into these areas? How might God be shaping you through these activities? Are there opportunities for relationships with others in which God might be encouraging you in these difficult areas? Pray through these.

The point of this exercise is to discern God's voice in *everything* on your to-do list. God may want to transform an undesirable obligation into a desirable obligation by changing your heart about it. The Lord may also want to reveal how your desires affect you; or he may show you the freedom you have to serve him, rather than allow your desire for prestige or power to dictate how you go about your work. God may desire to change you, to do something through you, or to reorient you to be a vessel of his grace to someone who needs it.

At the end of the practice, take a few minutes to pray over your day, your list, or your meeting. You could pray something like this:

> *God, I give back to you this [task, meeting, appointment, day]. I acknowledge you as the giver of my work, and I desire to honor you with it. Change me through my work today. Make me more into your likeness. Help me be attuned to your voice throughout this day, so I can follow what you have revealed to me about this [task, meeting, appointment, day]. Amen.*

Take two weeks to devote to trying this practice. If you consult your calendar only a couple of times a week or even once a week, you may want to try this practice over a longer period of time. What is important is regular repetition. Involving this practice in your regular work rhythms will help it be a meaningful and transformative practice for you.

# CALENDAR AND TO-DO LIST TRACKING ACTIVITY

Instructions: Pull out your calendar and to-do list. Look at what appointments you have and what tasks need to be finished over the course of the next week. Put the items on your list into these three categories:

*Desirable Obligations*. Things that you are obligated to do as part of your work responsibilities that you also enjoy.

*Desirable Options*. Things that are on your list not because you have to do them but simply because you want to do them.

*Undesirable Obligations*. Items that are required as a part of your work responsibilities but that you would not do if you had the choice. These things may not align well with your skill set, or they may involve interactions with people you find difficult, or they may simply be boring or repetitive.

| **Desirable Obligations** | **Desirable Options** | **Undesirable Obligations** |
| --- | --- | --- |

## QUESTIONS FOR REFLECTION OR DISCUSSION

1. *Have you ever incorporated prayer into the way you plan your work? If so, has it been helpful? How so? If not, why?*

2. *What motivations drive you in the tasks you place on your to-do list and calendar? (Your boss, money, family approval, personal motivation, and so on.)*

3. *From your list of Desirable Obligations, Desirable Options, and Undesirable Obligations, what stood out to you? Did the exercise reveal to you anything new about the ways in which you are motivated at work?*

4. *What place does God's agenda have in your work? Honestly assess this. How might you want it to change? How might God desire that to change?*

# 4

# READING SCRIPTURE AT WORK

How we think and what we think impacts the kind of people we become. We are influenced by the thought patterns of our minds on a daily and even moment-by-moment basis. As Christians, we have been given new minds and new hearts. So our thought patterns, the things we love, and how we act *should* be ruled and controlled by the Holy Spirit. But, as you know, it is not always that simple.

So many factors go into how we think, how we feel, and what we believe. Ultimately, what we believe will deeply affect who we are and how we behave in the workplace. How you live out at work who God has created you to be has a lot to do with what you believe. We all have deep-seated beliefs about who we are, what is important, and how we ought to live. These beliefs are impacted by many factors: the families within which we were brought up, the cultures that have shaped us, the belief systems our friends or church communities hold, and the work contexts in which we find ourselves. Each of these beliefs contributes to your thought patterns throughout the day, which in turn impacts the way you work, who you are at work, and how you treat others at work. If it sounds complicated, that's because it is.

The brain (the central place where thoughts and beliefs are formed) is a powerful tool. It has elasticity, which means that over time the things we think and do regularly change the neural pathways that run through our brain. Over time, the organ can change. This is seen negatively in conditions, such as dementia and Alzheimer's disease, but it can also be seen positively. The behaviors we regularly engage in and the thoughts we regularly return to have the power to change our brains and transform us.

This means that our minds *can* be changed and transformed. This is exactly what the apostle Paul was talking about when he said, "Do not conform to the pattern of this world but be transformed by the renewing of your mind. Then you will be able to test and approve what God's will is—his good, pleasing and perfect will" (Rom. 12:2). This transformation into people who live according to God's purpose in our day-to-day ordinary lives can start with becoming aware of our recurring thought patterns.

Psychologists have found that people have different mindsets. A growth mindset reflects the belief that we can change and grow, whereas a fixed mindset reflects the belief that our predispositions, personality traits, thought patterns, and abilities are stable and unchanging.[1] We can also have a growth or fixed mindset when it comes to our spiritual lives. We may believe that the Holy Spirit can change us into the people God has in mind for us to be—a spiritual growth mindset. Conversely, we may have a fixed mindset, believing that we will always be a certain way and have no agency to change and become new and different people.

## SETTING YOUR MIND ON CHRIST THROUGH SCRIPTURE

The apostle Paul is convinced that our spiritual renewal begins in the life of the mind. In his letter to the church at Ephesus, he echoes this sentiment when he writes:

> When you heard about Christ and were taught in him in accordance with the truth that is in Jesus. You were taught, with regard to your former way of life, to put off your old self, which is being corrupted by its deceitful desires; to be made new in the attitude of your minds; and to put on the new self, created to be like God in true righteousness and holiness. (Eph. 4:21–24)

Did you catch what Paul was saying? You can be made into a new kind of person by changing the attitude of your mind! But, in order for this to happen, our minds need renewal on a *daily basis*. The cultural philosophies of living, ways of functioning, and the common practices of those around us will shape how we think and act—especially at work. How we live out who God has created us to be, even at work, begins in the mind.

So how do we renew and change our minds and our behaviors? One of the most significant ways this can occur is through the regular reading of Scripture, putting the truth of God's word into our minds and meditating on it throughout the day. Whatever we set our minds on will be what guides our hearts and our behavior. Absorbing the truth of God's word sets our minds, hearts, and behaviors on a trajectory toward God's presence and guidance and, ultimately, toward the life God calls us to at work.

Many of us practice daily Scripture reading. We may read through the Psalms or read a passage from the Old and New Testaments each day. This is often done in the comfort of a favorite chair at home. Sometimes it is early in the day when the house is quiet, before the day gets going. Sometimes it is at night as we close out the day. There is nothing inherently wrong with reading Scripture this way, and there are many benefits to it. But it is limited.

Reading Scripture in your work or office space, however, can dramatically change not only how you read Scripture but also how you think about and engage in your work. Compare reading Scripture at work with reading it in the controlled environment of your home. At work, you cannot always control what happens. Reflecting on God's word *in* your workplace can help you see the context of Scripture differently. Reading Scripture in this environment will change the ways you work, how you interact with your coworkers, and how you are formed by God.

The impact of Jesus' teaching on loving your neighbor reads differently in your favorite chair at home, in front of the fireplace by yourself, than it does in your office when a coworker (with whom you have been clashing) walks by. Paul's teachings on the importance of reconciliation with God and his encouragement to be reconciled with others may be more impactful when we are at work and have an upcoming meeting with a difficult client or colleague. A psalm of lament affects us differently when we read it in a work environment that is causing us frustration, heartache, or longing.

## CALLED AT WORK

When Jesus called his disciples in Matthew 4, Mark 1, and Luke 5, he could easily have called them to follow him from their homes. He, of course, knew where each of them lived and was familiar with their comings and goings. But Jesus instead made a profound statement by visiting them *at work*. The first disciples' call to follow Jesus happened in the context of their livelihood—while they were dragging fishing nets in and out of their boats. The Gospel writers make a point to identify the work that Jesus' followers were doing before being called by Jesus. Simon Peter, Andrew, James, and John were fishermen. Matthew was a tax collector, and the Gospel writer Luke was a doctor. These mentions of vocation are not by chance in Scripture; they are intentional.

It is into the first disciples' work culture that Jesus arrives and brings a whole new way of thinking. He ushers in a new philosophy of living—a new way of being in the world—when he tells the disciples: *You've been fishing for fish. But now, I'm going to teach you how to fish for people* (see Matt. 4:19). Jesus uses the language of their work, the vocabulary of their vocations, to speak to them. And it is the same for us when we read Scripture in the context of our workplace.

What is astounding about the passage of the calling of these fishermen is that the disciples actually drop everything and follow Jesus. They leave everything for which they had trained, everything that was familiar, and everything that provided their livelihood—in order to follow Jesus! There was something absolutely compelling about the way Jesus called the first disciples that made them drop their nets and follow him. Maybe it was the fact that Jesus asked them to follow him—a countercultural move, as the tradition held that the disciple was the one who asked a rabbi to be his disciple. Or maybe it was a promise of a different life—one that did not involve the family business or shaking down people for taxes they could not afford. Or maybe it was the possibility of being a part of something revolutionary. Whatever it was, in the midst of their work, these first disciples heard the voice of the Savior. And when they chose to follow him, it completely changed the trajectory of their lives.

## LISTENING FOR THE VOICE OF THE SAVIOR

The lives of the disciples were never the same after hearing the voice of Jesus calling them to follow him. While they did not know the road ahead or even how they would be changed, hearing Jesus' call elicited in them a change of mind, heart, and action. This calling allowed them to participate with Jesus in ushering in a new kind of kingdom. Becoming fishers of people opened them up to a new way of thinking, loving, and being in the world.

Does the voice of the Savior have this kind of impact on you at work? Are you connected with Jesus in the midst of your work so that you hear the Lord's encouragement, guidance, and correction? Are you guided by the big and small calls of the Lord throughout your day? Do you hear the voice of the Savior on a daily basis?

It is clear from Scripture that if we want to be people who live according to the Spirit, then we will think about and set our minds on what the Spirit desires. Paul says it this way: "Those who live according to the flesh have their *minds* set on what the flesh desires; but those who live in accordance with the Spirit have their *minds* set on what the Spirit desires" (Rom. 8:5; emphasis added).

This type of attentiveness to God's Spirit is indeed possible. It is not out of reach, but it does require intention to live with attention. Setting our minds on the things of Christ requires a life steeped in Scripture. This type of life can begin with reading Scripture in your workspace. This does not mean you have to study it for hours on end or take a lot of time away from working to engage in this practice. It just takes ongoing and regular practice, until the practice becomes a habit.

You could choose to read a passage of Scripture when first arriving at work. Before you check your e-mail, attend your first meeting, walk to the factory floor, teach your students, or tend to your patients, you can put God's word in your mind and heart. Before something else catches your attention and takes up residence in your mind, you can orient yourself to hearing from God, changing the trajectory of your day as you allow yourself to be formed by Scripture in your workplace.

Another way of doing this is to read Scripture during a lunch break. You could do this in your workspace as a way of resetting your intentions toward God. Maybe you have had a hard morning, or you need clarity about a conversation you had. Reading Scripture at a lunch break can reset your mind and heart toward intentionally listening for God's voice in your work.

Some people may have the opportunity to read Scripture with colleagues at work. An increasing number of organizations have faith-based affinity groups, which allow employees to gather and read Scripture together at work. Not only hearing Scripture but having a community of coworkers to listen to and discuss Scripture within the context of your work could prove to be engaging, encouraging, and enlightening.

## "KEEP MY COMMANDS BEFORE YOU"

In the book of Deuteronomy, God commands the Hebrew people to keep his word at the forefront of their minds and hearts. Knowing how forgetful they can be, God tells them to keep his commands everywhere and rehearse them often. After having given them the Ten Commandments, which would keep them safely on the path of living a righteous life, God then says,

"These commandments that I give you today are to be on your hearts. Impress them on your children. Talk about them when you sit at home and when you walk along the road, when you lie down and when you get up. Tie them as symbols on your hands and bind them on your foreheads. Write them on the doorframes of your houses and on your gates." (Deut. 6:6–9)

Essentially, the Lord is saying to keep his words in your minds and hearts *always*. Not just in the morning before you get to work or at night when the day is ending. But keep God's word before you when you get up from and go back to bed, when you go out of buildings and into buildings, when you enter a room and when you leave a room, when you use your hands and your heads (your minds). This is a command to keep God's words close. If you do so, then what is in your mind reaches your heart and affects your behavior.

A way some Christians have done this at work is through placing Scripture in strategic places they will visit during the workday. For example, Scripture in the form of words or art may be placed next to or over the doorway of an office space. For those who spend a majority of their working hours in a vehicle, Scripture can be placed strategically on a dashboard or another place in the vehicle where it's easy to see and rehearse over and over.

Some people who work a lot on their computers use a biblical reference (such as "Romans8" or "Psalm23") as a password to unlock their computers. This is a good way to memorize a particular passage, especially when you pause after putting in the password and meditate on it, keeping God's words central in your thinking.

For those who work on their feet, carrying Scripture with you in a pocket may be a way to read it in your workspace. Writing some verses on an index card, wearing a bracelet or necklace with words on it, or holding some other symbol of God's word in a pocket may be a significant way to add Scripture to your working life.

If you prefer listening to reading, then these examples may not resonate with you. If that's the case, you may want to experience

Scripture at work through audio recordings. There is a fantastic soundtrack of the whole Bible called *The Bible Experience*.[2] Not only do actors read the Bible, but they also bring Scripture to life in a way that draws you into the immediacy of the biblical scene. This recording could be something that brings the Bible alive in your working life.[3] Listening to Scripture may be easier for those with the ability to listen to what they want at work in a private office or by using headphones. Some may find that listening to songs based on Scripture is a great way to keep God's word before them throughout the day. Since many hymns and worship songs incorporate the words of Scripture, by listening to them it becomes easy for you to memorize the words and go about your work with a song in your heart and mind.

## Lectio Divina

While reading Scripture once is a great way to get God's word in your mind, reading it multiple times allows it to sink deeply into your soul. An ancient practice called *lectio divina* ("divine reading") can aid you in this. This practice of reading Scripture with the expectation of hearing from God could make the word come alive for you. Here is how it works: You read through the same passage of Scripture three times, and each time you focus on something different.

The first time through, read the passage slowly and meditatively, allowing yourself to listen to the words of God as they are. Your goal is not to listen for anything specific but to pay attention the words as you hear them in your mind.

The second time you read, wait and listen for a word or a phrase from the passage to stand out to you. Do not force this word or phrase, and do not assume you will know what the word or phrase is in advance. You may be surprised at what stands out.

The third time you read, ask what God might be saying through that word or phrase for your workday. Then take that word or phrase with you throughout the day, coming back to it often, talking to God about it, and praying it over your work and your life. The podcast *Pray as You Go*,[4] which we mentioned in chapter 1, engages the practice of *lectio divina*. Experiment with the *lectio divina*. If you like to listen rather than read, this may be a good resource for you.

## STORIES OF THOSE WHO HAVE PRACTICED READING SCRIPTURE IN THE WORKPLACE

### *Dana's Story*

Dana is a nurse. Her work is long, intense, and often wrought with pain and suffering. Not only does she care for those who are suffering, but she also experiences suffering herself as she immerses herself in her work. Work is important to Dana, primarily because it takes up a significant amount of time in her life and because of its intense nature. Even though others recognize her work as a nurse as valuable, Dana does not love what she does. In the midst of her work, however, she has found a way to incorporate Scripture. This provides her with the perseverance, hope, and resiliency she needs to do her difficult job.

As a nurse, Dana is on her feet for long periods of time. For her, there is not much time (if any) for reflection and meditation. What she has found helpful, though, is writing a psalm on an index card and putting it in her pocket. As she touched the card during her shift, she was reminded of the words of the psalm and God's presence with her as she went about her duties. " 'I may not even read what I wrote [during my shift],' she explained, but because the psalms deal with 'suffering . . . that paper is a reminder that encourages me.' "[5]

This index card is a reminder to her of her faith in Jesus, a faith that provides her with the encouragement to keep going in the midst of a job she does not like and the intensity of emotions she encounters on a daily basis. This card was an Ebenezer of sorts, a symbol of remembering God's presence and a way to practice his command in Deuteronomy to always have his words before you. Carrying Scripture in her pocket at work was a way Dana could stay attuned to God and be faithful in her daily work.

## Michael's Story

Michael is the owner of a staffing firm in an urban area. He uses his business to provide employment to skilled workers, many of whom would not be able to find employment without the help, support, and infrastructure of a firm like his. When Michael first acquired his company, he had a lot of success built on one client. When that client left, Michael sought out the Lord's guidance, help, and direction. "In buying my company, I knew 'success' was not the endgame. I was following the Spirit—I wanted more of God. God was leading me to purchase this business, and so I followed. If I went down in flames, so be it. But, hopefully, I could do it in a way that brought glory to God."

Losing that client was the beginning of a time of refining for Michael, and both his faith and his business were challenged. "For me, [this business] has always been about the Lord." In fact, Michael views himself as being in full-time ministry as a businessman.

> It was my faith that drove me into business. I saw myself as a disciple of Jesus, stepping into business because the Holy Spirit was leading me that way. And trusting that he could make me the business person he needed me to be. At work, God has called me to pastor those people whom he identifies. I'm constantly asking, "Lord, is this person part of our flock?"

This is an unusual question in business, but Michael's consistent connection with God has provided a unique opportunity for him.

One of the ways Michael keeps this perspective is through reading Scripture at his desk prior to starting any other tasks for the day. This practice has sustained him through leaner times and provides a reminder to him that the end goal is not a dollar amount or prestige in his company. It is not even about providing jobs for those who need them the most, though that is a significant reason Michael does what he does. Rather, by reading Scripture in his workspace, Michael finds his priorities realigned each day, which allows him to see the goal of his work as serving people as Christ would.

This practice has also helped Michael break down the barriers between his "spiritual life" and his "working life." "There's no separation between sacred and secular," he says. "We can make spreadsheets to the glory of God, and we need wisdom for that. There's nothing too small that God doesn't care about it, and nothing too big that can't be better with the Lord's perspective." Having Scripture as the guiding factor in his day has changed the trajectory of his work, and it has expanded Michael's vision for what God is doing in his business.

## THE PRACTICE OF READING SCRIPTURE AT WORK

Reading Scripture in your workplace begins with intentionality. Forming a new habit can be difficult. If you are used to checking e-mail when you first arrive at work, then you may need to be intentional about choosing to let Scripture guide your mind and heart before you open your inbox. Consider when the best time might be in your workday to engage in this practice. Is it before work while you're still in your car? At your desk at the beginning of the day? Listening on headphones as you engage in manual tasks? During the lunch hour or another scheduled break time? You may find that you need to carve out time in your schedule to read Scripture. Being intentional about engaging this practice may mean putting it on your calendar so the tyranny of the urgent does not squeeze out the time you set aside to read Scripture at work.

If you work in a job where you are on your feet, without an office space or desk, you may need to be intentional about writing down a passage of Scripture and putting it somewhere you will see it, or in your pocket as you go about your day. It may be helpful to find audio recordings or Scripture in the form of songs you can listen to while working.[6] Whatever you need to engage in the practice of reading Scripture at work, be intentional about starting. Just start somewhere!

The Bible is filled with amazing stories, instructions, and parables, and it can be overwhelming at first to know where to begin. Below we provide three examples as a starting point for this practice. No matter which passage you begin with (or another of your choosing), read or listen slowly to it. Reading quickly in order to get through it and check the box will not reap the benefits of the practice. Reading slowly and allowing the words to sink in will help ensure that the words of Scripture penetrate deep into your heart and mind. Finally, pray that the Holy Spirit will illuminate what God is saying to you through this particular passage.

You may want to use the same passage for an entire week, familiarizing yourself with the words of a particular passage for a given amount of time. Or you may want to read through different consecutive passages in the course of a week. Whichever you choose, making this practice a part of your daily working rhythm can help you begin to pay attention to God's voice, be changed by the renewing of your mind, and be transformed into the worker God desires you to be.

## Psalm 23

This psalm of David, also known as the Shepherd Psalm, is a declaration that God is the one who provides. In this psalm, David provides poetic descriptions of God bringing him provision, rest, security, blessing, and protection from his enemies. When read in your workspace, this psalm can deepen your experience of and trust in God. It may also bring an awareness of the Lord's presence in your own work.

Read this psalm slowly. In your mind, picture the rich imagery it portrays. Think about what drinking from a quiet pool might look like for you. What would a feast in the presence of your enemies be like? What is the goodness that God has brought to you today?

As you read, pay attention to your surroundings. Think about this psalm in the context of your work. Think about your tasks and the people with whom you work. What might God have to say to you today through Psalm 23 for these tasks, in this setting, with these people?

### Proverbs 31

The book of Proverbs is packed with instructions on wise living, and Solomon does not skimp on talking about work. Many of the instructions in Proverbs can be readily applied to your work. Proverbs contains warnings about staying on the path that God has designed and it also provides exhortations to seek wisdom.

In Proverbs 31, we find the example of a "Valiant Worker."[7] While this passage has been used primarily as an example for wives, it is a useful passage for anyone who works. The woman described works willingly, joyfully, and with wisdom. Both men and women, married or single, can learn from her example what it looks like to work for the glory of God.

As you read through this passage think about the example of the Valiant Worker. What is the example she has set for us? How can you work likewise with diligence and her level of planning, joy, and willingness?

As you read, pay attention to your surroundings. Think about this chapter in the context of your work. Think about your tasks and the people with whom you work. What might God have to say to you today through Proverbs 31 in this setting, for these tasks, with these people?

## Romans 12

In the book of Romans, Paul provides an explanation of the miracle of the gospel of grace as well as instructions for how to live in light of this miracle. In Romans 12, he encourages the Christians in Rome to "set their lives before God as an offering" (Rom. 12:1–2). As we explored in chapter 3, "Surrendering the Calendar," this call to offer ourselves to God has many applications to the workplace. Because of the grace of God, we too can give our everyday lives back to God as living sacrifices who desire to bring glory to God.

Later in chapter 12, Paul outlines what this life of sacrifice to God looks like. It entails a life lived in love toward others—both those who love you back and those who love to hate you. It also instructs us to live in harmony and agreement with one another, associating with people in positions different from yours, and overcoming evil with good. This is an especially helpful passage to reflect on for those in positions of leadership at work. There is much to glean from this one chapter (and even more from the whole book of Romans!). Take several days to read and reread it in your workspace, asking the Holy Spirit to bring to mind this chapter throughout your day and make you into a person for whom the traits encouraged by Paul become a reality.

As you read, pay attention to your surroundings. Think about this chapter in Roman in the context of your work. Think about your tasks and the people with whom you work. What might God have to say to you today through Romans 12 for these tasks, in this setting, with these people?

## QUESTIONS FOR REFLECTION OR DISCUSSION

1. *Have you ever read Scripture in the workplace? What was that experience like? If not, why not? What might that look like for you?*

2. *How might the context and application of Scripture change for you if you were to bring it into your workplace?*

3. *After having tried the practice, how did it go? What worked? What didn't work? What did you notice about yourself, your surroundings, and your work as a result of participating in the practice?*

4. *When would be a good time to continually practice this in the workplace? How will you engage over the next month in this practice so it becomes a habit?*

# PART TWO

# Engaging in Work

As we're well aware, the bulk of our daily lives is spent working. For many of us, engaging in the work we are called to do involves our whole selves and our undivided attention. Our work requires us to be present, attentive, creative, and productive. When we work, we become problem solvers, artists, and craftspeople, using our ingenuity and capacity for making something out of seemingly nothing or taking something that exists and making it better.

This language may be foreign to you, as you think about your work. "I'm a truck driver. How in the world is there an art to driving a truck?" or "I'm a house cleaner," or "I'm a customer service agent. How can my engagement of work be like something a craftsman does?" This requires a fresh way of looking at your job. You need to see your occupation in the light of the God who called you to this work—to see it as a *vocation*, a divine call. Your identity as a worker, whatever the job, is shaped first and foremost by whom God calls you to be.

As we looked at the book of Genesis in the introduction, we saw that when God first created Adam and Eve, he created in them in his image and likeness. This was their true identity: first, they were God's image bearers; and second, God gave them specific work to do. Both are parts of their identity. Adam and Eve were not only made in the image and likeness of the Creator, but they were also given work to do as a reflection of who they were as people.

On this point, Tim Keller and Katherine Leary Alsdorf write,

> We see God not only working, but commissioning workers to carry on his work. . . . [God] tells human beings to "fill the earth and subdue it." . . . The word "subdue" indicates that, though all God had made was good, it was still to a great degree undeveloped. God left creation with a deep untapped potential for cultivation that people were to unlock in their labor.[1]

So, yes, engaging in work means that we reflect the image of God; and by engaging in work, we become co-creators in the work of subduing creation—making something new, as artists, crafts-people, and problem solvers.

The practices in this section are to help you reflect God as his image bearer, becoming more like God; but, they are also for the sake of the work itself. We pray that as you go about your work that you may be changed to reflect more of who God is as a worker, for the sake of others.

In this section, "Engaging in Work," we explore four spiritual practices:

1. ***Affirmation of Calling***. *Asking God to speak his love and acceptance over you throughout the day can transform your motivations and identity at work, which in turn will change your performance and work relationships in a variety of ways.*

2. ***Gratitude and Celebration***. *Expressing gratefulness by consciously affirming God's blessings and others' contributions to our lives can help us avoid hubris and develop appropriate humility. When we choose to celebrate the work*

*of God and others, we diminish the sense that we are the source of all goodness or our own success.*

3. **Confession at Work.** *In the practice of confession, we admit where we have contributed to the brokenness in our world, our work, and our organizations. In confessing where we fall short at work, we allow God to transform our work as we are molded and shaped as Christian workers.*

4. **Lamenting Work**. *When we bring our laments about work to God, we give him the space to bring correction where we may have contributed to the heartbreak and frustration. We also give God the space to do what only he can do—heal and bring newness and hope.*

# 5

# AFFIRMATION OF CALLING

For many of us, our work is tied to our identity. It makes sense that it would be. We identify ourselves with where we spend our time, energy, and passions. One of the first questions we ask people when we meet them is, "What do you do?" It seems as though we identify each other through work as well: She's a professor. He's an airplane mechanic. She works for a start-up. He owns a coffee shop. She drives a delivery truck. He is an accountant—and so on. This is not necessarily a bad thing. It is a way of identifying one aspect of who people are. But we must take a hard look at the ways in which our working identities form us. If we are not careful, the identity we have from our work can become an idol that moves us away from what God wants to do for us and through us.

As anyone who has ever lost a job knows, work comes and goes, and it can change with different seasons. To have our sense of self so wrapped up in a job or a title can be destructive to us and how we operate in the workplace. At the same time, work *is* important. It is built into the fabric of creation and assigned to Adam and Eve from the very beginning. God tells the first humans to be fruitful, to multiply, and to "rule over the fish in the sea and the birds in the sky and over every living creature that moves on the ground" (Gen. 1:28b). Their responsibilities, however, didn't end there. They were also told to care for and cultivate all of the trees and plants of the earth (Gen. 1:30). The first humans were given all of creation to care for, live in, develop, and make something of. In short, God gives humans the responsibility to build civilization and culture.

We are designed to work for the good of the world. These God-ordained responsibilities are known as the "creation mandate."

Sandwiched between God's creation of people and the instruction he gave them to steward creation, there is a short phrase that is easy to gloss over and miss. Three words appear immediately before this creation mandate: "God blessed them" (Gen. 1:28a). *God. Blessed. Them.* In Scripture, a blessing is a verbal word spoken over someone, invoking God's Spirit to bring about something good. A blessing is a type of prayer, but it is more than that: it calls upon the goodness, energy, and action of the Holy Spirit to make something new happen. While today we often ask for physical or material blessings, in the Old Testament blessings primarily communicate identity. They are words that convey our relationship with the Creator. The first blessing in Scripture identifies human beings as chosen and set apart by God, first and foremost. Yes, we are people given the work of making something of the created order; but before that, we belong to the Lord.

## THE BLESSING OF GOD

When the people of God escaped from Egypt, God established a covenant with them. This covenant was a promise of God's blessing, always. It is this blessing that the Lord gave to the priests to speak to the people on God's behalf. This blessing was not based on physical provision but on the Hebrews' *relationship* with God. The Lord said to Moses,

> "Tell Aaron and his sons, 'This is how you are to bless the Israelites.' Say to them: 'The LORD bless you and keep you; the LORD make his face shine on you and be gracious to you; the LORD turn his face toward you and give you peace.' So, they will put my name on the Israelites, and I will bless them." (Num. 6:22–27)

It was with the Lord's own name that the people were to be identified. This blessing communicated God's goodness and graciousness to the Israelites, and his attentiveness to their needs and ability to quell all their fears with peace. The blessing was a way of reminding the Israelites of their identity in relation to the Father. As a people chosen by the Lord, they could rest in the fact that God held their lives together. It is God who brings goodness. It is God who provides for their needs. It is God who reveals who they were created to be and who ushers in peace when it is needed most.

Do you see the purpose of these blessings? The blessing conveyed the ways God turned the people toward not just who they are but *whose* they are. We can see it in God's blessing at creation and in the blessing when the nation of Israel was being established. It was as if God was shouting: *Know whose you are before you go and do anything!* Know whose you are before you work to make something of the world, before you interact with other nations, before you establish any other identity: *Know whose you are.*

## YOU TOO BELONG TO GOD

It is the same for us today. Each day we rise and live our lives, seeking to make sense of and to make something of what we have been given. We are culture makers and shapers. We are creative and curious. We are teachers, builders, scientists, salespeople, caretakers, pastors, artists, engineers, designers, manufacturers, servers, doctors, postal workers, chefs, parents, and spouses. But before that, *we* are God's people: chosen, provided for, showered in goodness and grace, and covered by God's peace. Before we are given callings and vocations, roles and responsibilities, we are first given the blessing of belonging to God.

As a people chosen by the Lord, we can rest in the fact that it is God who holds our lives together. It is God who brings goodness to our lives. It is God who provides for our needs. It is God who ushers in peace when it's needed most. This is our first identity. We are God's.

When we identify ourselves with our work first, we get wrapped up in what we do rather than in whose we are. But when we are grounded in our identity as children of God, our work isn't an avenue for proving ourselves but rather a space in which we can live out the love and connection we have with God. As people blessed by God, we are called to live out that blessing in every part of our lives, including our work.

This can be hard to do. Our attention is pulled in many different directions, especially at work. Our motivations for working get muddled, we get frustrated with our work, and we can experience pain in our work, casting shadows on the goodness we experience. But there's a remedy for our distraction and waywardness. The remedy is for us to be grounded in the love, blessing, and goodness of God, who protects our hearts and minds from finding our primary value in what we do rather than in who we are.

## ACCEPTED BEFORE WE PRODUCE

Asking God to speak his love and acceptance over you throughout the day can transform your motivations and identity at work. This in turn will change your performance and work relationships in a variety of ways. When we know we are accepted before the workday begins, no matter what happens in our work that day, a transformation takes place. Instead of being driven by the fear that we will not measure up, we work because we are loved by Christ. There is nothing we need to prove.

This is easier said than done. Most of us need to be rooted in our identity in God and his love on a daily basis. This is not a one-time understanding that we learn at some point and then automatically enact forevermore. It is something we need to be reminded of every day. If we are not grounded in the fact that we are loved with the everlasting love of God *before* we give the presentation, *before* we make the sale, *before* we have the performance review, *before* we are commended or criticized at work, then our work can become motivated by anxiety, fear, and a desire to prove ourselves as competent and capable. When fear is the motivation, we measure ourselves by our performance at work. We feel acceptance when we are well liked or given positive feedback. Conversely, we can enter into self-loathing when we are criticized or lectured on what we have done wrong.

On the other hand, being grounded in who God says we are has incredible implications for how we think about ourselves, what we believe about ourselves, and how we act at work. Remember in the previous chapter how your beliefs and thoughts shape your mindset and therefore your behavior? Believing you are loved by God prior to *doing* anything in the day has the power to reinforce the blessing of God in your life. When we are grounded in God's love and blessing, we more readily hear the voice of the Savior claiming us and guiding us. By being in communion with God and asking on a regular basis, "What do you want me to do here and now?" the Lord's calling becomes a natural overflow of a God-shaped identity. Responding to those calls in trust and obedience is something we can practice over and over again as we hear the voice of the Good Shepherd.

## THREE KINDS OF CALLINGS

### *The General Call*

To be called by God means we hear the voice of God leading us in both a general and a particular direction. On the one hand, every Christ follower has the same general calling: to experience God's love and saving grace poured out on us, and to live a life of obedience to God through the power of the Holy Spirit. If you have accepted the forgiveness and grace available through Jesus, then you have experienced this general calling, which is common to each faithful disciple. We are called to be in close relationship with the

Savior, moment by moment receiving the Lord's guidance and direction. We are called to love our neighbors as ourselves.

Doug Koskela, a theology professor and author of the book, *Clarity and Calling*, explains it this way,

> All are called to a life of prayer, whether or not you discern that you have a particular gift of prayer. Each of us has a responsibility to bear good news to the world in both word and deed, whether or not you have a particular gift of evangelism. In the same way, you are not called to love God and your neighbor only if you feel like it. Rather, you are called to such love even when—perhaps especially when—it's difficult and painful.[1]

### The Particular Calling

Each of us has the same general calling, but the particular ways in which it is expressed will be as different as each person is from the next. The Puritans referred to this as the "particular call," while others have referred to it as a "missional call," because it reflects the way our own unique circumstances, talents, passions, and opportunities come together to provide an overall purpose or guiding mission for life.[2] Each person's particular call includes all of the roles and tasks that are unique to them and done in service to God and others. These distinctive callings can change over time and reflect the conditions and obligations that we have in a given season in life or moment in time. If we are married, then we are called to love and faithfulness in that marriage. If we have children, then we are called to nurture them and raise them to know God. If we are employed, then we are called to do our work diligently and with integrity—and to rest regularly. We have particular callings associated with the fact that we are in relationship with particular colleagues, neighbors, and church communities.

You can think of the general call as one that requires us to set a course in a direction toward faithfulness to Christ. The particular call comes when we choose a path to take toward this general direction. As you walk down this path, you may come to an intersection where you have a choice to make—not between being faithful or not, but rather *how* you should be faithful. At this point, you can rely on God's direction to know which path to take. The grace that is imparted to you may come through your role in your family. Or perhaps you might experience God's direction and love through a relationship at work. The particular calling finds its manifestation in partnership with the general call.

## The Direct Call

In addition to the general and particular calls, there is a third kind of call we see in Scripture, where God calls a specific person to do a specific task at a specific time. Doug Koskela refers to these specific callings from God as a "direct call."[3] Moses was called to lead the Hebrew people out of Egypt. Jonah was called to preach to the people of Nineveh. Mary was called to be the mother of Jesus. Jewish Peter was called to eat with Cornelius the gentile. Saul, the persecutor of the church, was called to join the first-century Christians. Unlike particular callings, the direct call may or may not correspond with someone's skill set or interests. Moses had a speech impediment, and yet God called him to confront Pharaoh and lead his people. Jonah had no desire to bring God's message to the Ninevites, the enemies of Israel. And Saul was more interested in persecuting Christians than joining them. Nonetheless, God gave each of them a direct call, along with the power to carry it out.

While we see God using these types of direct calls throughout all of Scripture, these stand out because they are unusual, and because they often run counter to our expectations of what would be suitable for a particular person. Of course, most people, even those who are faithful Christians, don't encounter blinding lights from heaven. When such a call does occur, however, it is quite obvious (a burning bush! a pregnant virgin!); and God empowers the person to accomplish the call, often in spite of their gifts, talents, proclivities, or interests. Those who experience direct calls may be surprised and perhaps even dismayed by them, as Moses was upon receiving his call to lead the Hebrews to freedom.

When God gave leadership, a position of power, and an assignment to Moses, Moses did not respond with jubilation.[4] Instead he entered into a conversation with God: *What you have given me is too hard, God!* From Moses' perspective, the responsibility God gave him to lead the people out of Egypt into the Promised Land was overwhelmingly daunting. *I'm not qualified. I'm not the right man for this job. Someone else will do a better job.* Because Moses had entered into a conversation with God, he displayed an openness to hearing God's response.

Have you ever been asked to step into a role, a job, or a task that seemed way above your pay grade? Have you received a direct call from God that seems out of your league, or way above your pay grade? Have you found yourself in a position you never would have asked to be in, and yet God seemed to use you despite your limitations? If so, you are in the company of Moses himself!

The key to Moses' success was not just that God's power backed him, although that certainly carried him a long way. Moses steps into his direct calling, because he admitted his limitations and postured himself with an openness to hear from God, to be molded by God, and accept the vocation God had placed on his life, *in spite of his doubt.* If you receive a direct calling on your life, it may not initially make sense. But take the calling seriously and enter into God's calling on your life despite your hesitation because God's direct calling always aligns with a person's God-given identity.

## DISCERNING THE CALL

When people wonder about what God is calling them to do, it is typically not the direct call about which they are confused: The direct call is clear and obvious, and there may be conversation with God involved, but the calling itself is clear. Neither is there often confusion about the general call: It is not hard to understand that God calls each believer to faithful discipleship and to love and serve others. Rather, when people ask what God is calling them to, they are usually wondering about their *particular callings*.

So how do I know what my particular calling is? Most of the time, this question is raised in the context of a particular decision that needs to be made. What college should I go to? What should I major in? What job should I take? Whom should I date or marry? Should I change careers? Should I rent or buy? Should I move? We often try to discern our particular calling in a way that reflects a relatively unique historical time and place, where the answers to these questions are not foreordained.

For many centuries, it did not occur to people to ask these questions, because they did not have choices about education, a career, marriage, or where they lived, and so on. They followed a particular path, because it was the only one available. While we today often focus our attention on trying to figure out what God is calling us to in these domains, most of Scripture doesn't seem concerned with helping us figure out these particularities. Instead, Scripture emphasizes the importance of knowing the voice of God. That does not mean we shouldn't pay attention to our interests and skills, our experiences and background, or the gifts the Holy Spirit gives us—any of these ways may be how God speaks to us! But there are other ways for us to hear God's voice to which we need to pay attention. We need first to learn how to *listen* for this voice, to continually ask what God wants us to know and do.

In order to know the voice of the Savior in our particular callings, we must recognize the voice of the Savior in our general calling. First, we get to know God's voice through the words of Scripture. The biblical writers illuminate God's character; and through their writings, we can begin to understand God's desires for the world and for its people.

Second, we get to know God's voice of direction through prayer. Prayer is the vehicle through which God speaks in particular ways to each of us. Getting to know the voice of the Good Shepherd takes time and patience. The more we listen, hear, and obey the voice of the Savior, the more we discern God's purposes in our lives and understand our unique identity.

Third, we get to know God's voice through other faithful people, who have listened to God and who have lived accordingly. These voices may be found in our local church community, our fellowship with other Christians, and through reading or hearing the words of saints throughout the ages who have paid attention to God's general and specific callings in their lives.

Seeking the voice of God in these three ways helps us become familiar with God's voice, so that in the midst of our particular callings, we can hear that voice clearly. This does not always make the particular callings easy—like the mothers and fathers of the faith before us, we may be called to difficult things.

Generally, any particular call will bring with it things to celebrate and things to lament, things to embrace and things that are more difficult to live out. This is the Christian life. Although it may not always be easy, we are still called to faithfulness to Christ *in all things*. Trusting Christ is a part of our general calling, which we can live out as we receive our particular callings. For instance, each of us is called to be a disciple—one who follows the ways of Christ in humility and love. Who we love and where we express humility will depend on the people with whom we interact on a daily basis in our particular callings.

How one person relates to their spouse and children will (hopefully) be within the bounds of love and grace from the general call; but what is loving to each family member can be discerned only in the confines of that person's specific calling to their family. One person's relationships and activity at work will be lived out differently than another's because each work situation is different. It is in our particular call that we live out our general call. The call to love is the same for every Christian, but my call (Denise) to teach my students well and conduct research with diligence and integrity is different from another professor's approach; and my call (Shannon) to love and teach my kids and be in partnership with my husband, in my particular ways, are just for me.

Some of the people God calls you to love may be a joy to be around. If that is the case, then embrace it. On the other hand, some of those with whom you are called to love and work may be more difficult. They may cause you to lament and grieve; nevertheless, you are still called to live out your general calling to follow the ways of Christ and your particular calling to that specific difficult person. It is easy when we have people in our lives who are wonderful to be around—of course, I'm called to be in relationship with them! It is easy when we have a job that is a perfect fit for our skills, personality, and experience—obviously God has called me to this! But what happens when relationships are difficult, when work is just so-so or worse, and we feel stuck and frustrated? Does that mean God is calling us to something different? Maybe, but not always.

Sometimes we are called into a deeper obedience *especially* when it gets hard. Sometimes God desires us to be fully committed to him in obedience, even when it does not make sense to us. Working out of a sense of obedience to God is much more fulfilling than working out of an obligation to a boss. Working in obedience allows our spiritual vision to focus on what God might be doing in the midst of frustration, conflict, or unfair conditions. This takes discernment. Knowing whether you are to stay or go when faced with less than ideal circumstances at work requires you to lean in close to the Savior to hear what you need to hear during these seasons.

Discerning a call to move in a different direction, to stay where you are, or to change some behaviors in a relationship, position, or vocation can be challenging. It is a process that usually takes time. Sometimes God calls us to go, to move on to the next adventure. But sometimes we are called to stay. God is more concerned about your character in a given situation than in your circumstances. Relying on circumstances alone to determine God's call may be misleading and cause you to miss what is most important.

Knowing the voice of God in your general calling helps you clearly hear God's voice in the particular callings of your life. If on a daily basis you hear the Lord's nudges, his affirmation of love for you, and his wisdom for living your daily life, then you will notice and hear God's callings in the specifics of your life as well. But if you haven't come to know the voice of the Savior in the general callings—the call to discipleship, love, and justice—then it will be harder for you to hear and respond to God's voice when the calling toward different vocations comes.

## LEARN TO PAY ATTENTION

Learning to pay attention to our everyday lives is essential in the tasks of answering the particular calls placed on us. Seeking to hear the voice of God is an exercise to be practiced over and over again. It is the regular, moment-by-moment acknowledgment of the presence of God in our lives, tasks, and interactions that trains our hearts toward knowing the voice of the Good Shepherd and allowing the shepherd's crook of wisdom to guide our days. It is in the moment-by-moment listening to God's voice that we learn how to know what to do.

Following God's general callings will lead to the particular calling God has placed on your life. Discerning your particular calling, though, requires for you to have a combination of knowing God, community affirmation, scriptural consistency, and an alignment with who God created you to be.

Many people have found the following guiding questions helpful as particular callings come into question:

- *Is the direction in which I am being led consistent with what we know of God in Scripture?*

- *Is this calling consistent with what I am hearing from God directly?*

- *Is this calling consistent with feedback from the community of faith?*

- *Is what I sense as God's direction consistent with who God has created me to be?*

If the answer to these questions is yes, then most likely you are being led toward a particular calling. If the answer is no to some of the questions, you may need to continue to discern the direction in which you are to go. There are other times when God says, "You pick!" You can live out a faithful life as a disciple in both jobs you have been offered, at both colleges you were accepted to, and so on. While discernment is an important process, the particularities of living out our discipleship are not as important as actually living out our discipleship. You could love your next-door neighbor here or your next-door neighbor in the state you are thinking about moving to. What God desires is for you to be faithful in all seasons.

## DISCERNMENT WHEN THERE IS NO CHOICE

We would be remiss if we did not mention that many people have no choice about work, education, or living circumstances. You work the job you have because it provides for your needs and the needs of your family. It is the only job available and so you do it. Those in that situation, however, can still hear God's affirmation of calling. You may not have a choice in your work, but you have freedom in Christ to experience the love of God and fellowship of the Holy Spirit in your work, and to live out the identity you have been given—no matter what kind of job you have. You can hear the "well done" of the Lord, despite work that is mind-numbingly repetitive. You can hear the affirmation of whose you are, regardless of what your daily tasks entail. Lean in and allow your work to be an offering to God, working "at it with all your heart, as working for the Lord, not for human masters" (Col. 3:23).

## RENEWAL OF CALLING

Once we have answered our particular call to a specific path, we can be tempted to forget how God led and guided us. We can get into the routine of work and life, taking for granted what we have heard along the way from God. We get into conflict with a coworker and wonder, "God called me to this, but did I hear the calling right?" When work does not live up to our expectations, we can be left with disappointment and be tempted toward despair. We ask ourselves, "Am I still called to this job?" When we encounter these doubts and skepticism about our abilities to hear God, and we wonder about our longevity in a given relationship or role, we may find the need to hear the renewal of calling from God.

This affirmation may come as a still small voice encouraging you: "I've called you to this." It may come from a surprising comment made by a boss or coworker. You may hear "Thank you," or "We need you on this team." It may come from the reality that God continues to provide for you financially through your work. When these affirmations come during seasons of doubt, pay attention to them. They may be God speaking blessing over you.

There may be other times when these small nudges are not enough. The discouragement has become too much, the heartbreak in your work too apparent, and the lament too long. When this happens, you may need to add some of the other practices to your discernment process. Practices like the prayer of examen for work and solitude may be helpful during these times. (These will be discussed in detail in subsequent chapters.) Also, bringing a discerning community of trusted friends, mentors, and pastors alongside your decisions can help in bearing the weight of the discernment process.

If you are in a season of needing a renewal of calling, know this: You are not alone. God sees you, hears you, and he is with you in the pain of it. Seek God in this season, and listen for where God's voice leads.

## STORIES OF AFFIRMATION OF CALLING

### *Karen's Story*

Karen has worked in a variety of settings—as a registered nurse, a parent educator at a community college, a high school teacher of students with special needs, and more recently in nonprofit leadership roles. She found her calling, not in a particular career or job, but rather in listening to discern *who* God created her to be. Her calling is primarily that of identity. This emphasis on identity came into focus one day when a friend told her, "You know you're a pastor, right?" Karen responded with a bit of confusion, since her job titles had never included the word *pastor*! Her friend then explained that Karen interacted with others in her life in a pastoral way, saying, "It's not your job, but it is who you are."

Karen never forgot those words. Over the following years, she learned to ask God for more specific words about who he created her to be. And through various times of prayer focused on listening to God, she has heard the following aspects of her identity: loving pastor, curious shepherd, healer of souls. She says that often her first inclination is to reject these names, but over time she has become convinced that God has specific words for each of us about our identities. As she lives into these names, she experiences a new joy and freedom—a freedom not to compare or measure herself against others, but to live into who God created her to be. Her current work involves the opportunity to disciple women of various ages, and she finds joy in watching God transform their lives as they too discover who God created them to be, no matter what their work setting. As Karen says, "When we realize that our particular identities have been chiseled into God's kingdom, we recognize how critical it is to ask God, who created us intricately in our mother's womb, to reveal to us all that he created us to be."

## Anna's Story

As the director of admissions for a small Christian college, it was Anna's primary responsibility to recruit students. One morning, she received a call from a student who had recently been denied admission. In the past, these had been some of her least favorite conversations, mostly because Anna wanted to focus her limited time on working with potential students. But after going through a yearlong, church-based course focused on integrating her faith and her work, she came to believe that her job had an importance beyond the university where she worked, and that she had the potential to impact her community and higher education in general. Anna had been reflecting on the idea that God cared about her meeting her employer's expectations, as well as her efforts toward positive outcomes beyond her employer.

This idea broadened Anna's perspective on the scope and purpose of her work, and she felt God prompting her to meet this student for a face-to-face conversation. When the young man walked into her office, at first he would not make eye contact with Anna and mumbled his words softly. They met only for a matter of minutes, but Anna encouraged his pursuit of higher education even though that journey would not be with this particular university. As she talked more about the variety of routes that were open to him, he began to look her in the eye. By the time he left, it was obvious he had regained much of his confidence in himself and his future. He had received an affirmation of calling of sorts, through Anna's words to him. While his higher education would not be at this particular university, God used Anna to encourage and to clarify to this young man that he should not give up the desire to get his degree.

Although this meeting did not get her any closer toward her goal of recruiting new students, Anna recognized the positive impact it might have outside of the university. By meeting with this young man, Anna gave him the confidence he needed to continue to pursue an education, which would benefit him, his family, and ultimately the community. Following this encounter, Anna made a habit of evaluating her priorities and considering the impact of her decisions on constituents beyond her university. This interaction provided her with a clarification and expansion of her own particular calling—not only was her work to be done well for her employer, but she could also encourage and promote wellness in the lives of those who never attended her university. After this, she began to consider the impact her workplace activities might have on the local community and, more broadly, in higher education. As a result, she participated in initiatives that benefitted students, families, and her colleagues in ways that extended beyond the narrow scope of her primary role as a recruiter.

## Paul's Story

Paul was born and raised in the United Kingdom and moved with his wife to the United States in his early thirties. God seemed to be heralding a new chapter in his vocational journey, calling Paul to shift from his work in the advertising world and move into strategic consulting. In the States, Paul became well established in his new community, built a successful consulting practice, and settled into full-time work. Several years later, he began working part time as the workplace pastor in a local, large Pentecostal church. God appeared to be blessing Paul's work. His start-up had grown from a vision into an established organization, and his pastoral role, which had begun as something of an experiment, was now a fully functioning position in the church.

After some time, Paul describes a sense of "holy unrest" that filled his work. During a conference, he encountered a guest speaker from his homeland. As this speaker shared about his own work and calling, it became apparent that God might have something in store in a completely different setting back in the UK. This came as a surprise, because returning there was the last thing on Paul's bucket list of must-do! But during this conversation, something awoke in

Paul, and he began to see possibilities he had not previously considered. Numerous events occurred that seemed to imply it was time to return to the UK—specifically, people who were not aware of the circumstances expressed that God might be calling Paul home.

He describes three things that aligned in the months he and his wife were processing what God was saying and how they should respond. First, they embedded themselves in God's word, trying to discern God's direction. Second, they were attentive to what the Holy Spirit was saying to them as they prayed. And third, they sought out wise counsel of people they trusted. After a significant time of prayer, Paul's wife told him, "This is it! I believe God has been preparing us for this. He is calling us to return and make a difference in our homeland at this time, where there is a bigger need that ever for the gospel in the culture."

A number of other factors affirmed their decision to move. Paul was sought out by a British charity and offered a position that would take advantage of his experience as a pastor and also as a business leader. As he was considering the opportunity, he met with a former British MP and lord in the Houses of Parliament. This man affirmed for Paul the value of the role he had been asked to take on, and his perspective carried a sense of affirmation and commissioning. This British lord took Paul to the Chapel of St. Mary Undercroft in the Palace of Westminster and prayed a commissioning prayer over him. It was a beautiful experience of hearing God's direction for the calling Paul had received.

## PRACTICE OF THE AFFIRMATION OF CALLING

### General Call

The practice of the affirmation of calling happens in two ways. First, there is an affirmation of whose we are. Who we belong to, how loved we are, and God's presence in the ordinary elements of our lives are all things we need to be reminded of daily (sometimes hourly). These affirmations deal with our general calling—our calling to be the beloved of God and to act out of our own belovedness.

The affirmation of our general calling happens when we are intentional about reminding ourselves of what Scripture says about us and about who God is. One way to practice this is to set a timer to go off two to three times a day (but not when you would interrupt important meetings or tasks with others at work). Each time the timer goes off, use it as a moment to pause and remind yourself of whose you are and who you are from God's perspective. You could read a Scripture passage that affirms this or say a simple prayer, asking God to speak love over you and your work.

A second way to do this is to let your everyday work rhythms be a reminder of the affirmation that you are loved and accepted by God, regardless of how work goes that day. It may be an intentional pause as you swipe a key card to get into a building. It may be an intentional pause while your students are at recess or while a doctor is checking out the patient in your care. It may be each time you change a diaper for the toddlers with whom you spend your days. You know when those pauses can take place in your work, so be intentional about hearing that affirmation multiple times a day.

## Particular Call

Unlike the daily affirmation of general calling, an affirmation of our particular callings can take much longer to discern or hear. We may begin to discern our particular callings first through reading Scripture. Knowing the God of Scripture can help us align our decisions with the Lord's character. Prayer is another path of discernment. Wrestling with God through the ins and outs of vocational change ensures God's presence in our decisions. Third, trusted people in our faith community can help with discernment. People who know you well can see things you cannot. Ask for godly wisdom and guidance, as well as people to join with you in prayer over these big decisions. Finally, asking good questions can help lead you toward the path you should take. (At the end of this chapter, we provide a number of reflection and discussion questions for you to consider.)

Hearing the affirmation of God upon a particular calling can give us the confidence to go forward—even if it is difficult or not what we would automatically choose for ourselves. God's affirmation can propel us into work that brings glory to the Lord and blessing to the people around us.

When you are in the process of seeking God's affirmation toward a vocational direction, you can feel lonely and question why God is not answering. The following encouragement from Pierre Teilhard de Chardin may be helpful in this season:

> *Above all, trust in the slow work of God.*
> *We are quite naturally impatient in everything*
> *to reach the end without delay.*
> *We should like to skip the intermediate stages.*
> *We are impatient of being on the way to something*
> *unknown, something new.*
> *And yet it is the law of all progress*
> *that it is made by passing through*
> *some stages of instability—*
> *and that it may take a very long time.*
> *And so I think it is with you;*
> *your ideas mature gradually—let them grow,*
> *let them shape themselves, without undue haste.*
> *Don't try to force them on,*
> *as though you could be today what time*
> *(that is to say, grace and circumstances*
> *acting on your own good will)*
> *will make of you tomorrow.*
> *Only God could say what this new spirit*
> *gradually forming within you will be.*
> *Give Our Lord the benefit of believing*
> *that his hand is leading you,*
> *and accept the anxiety of feeling yourself*
> *in suspense and incomplete.*[5]

## QUESTIONS FOR REFLECTION OR DISCUSSION

Review and examine your own life.

1. *How have you heard God's general calling in your life?*

2. *When have you heard a particular call from God in your life?*

3. *What is your current particular calling?*

4. *When have you needed a reaffirmation of God's calling on your life?*

5. *What are your particular talents? From whom have you received positive feedback about your skills or abilities?*

6. *What do you enjoy in your daily work? What do you enjoy outside of your daily work? Is there a call in these tasks that bring you delight?*

7. *What needs are you most aware of in your workplace? In your larger community? How could you perhaps help meet those needs?*

8. *Is there someone in your life you think can help you discern your calling?*

9. *What have you heard from the Holy Spirit regarding what may be next for you?*

# 6

# GRATITUDE AND CELEBRATION

Success may be one of the most spiritually fraught experiences we can have. It is easy when things are going well to think that our own skills and talents are the reason for our good outcomes. Maybe you have seen the quotes floating around that promote believing in yourself and working hard as ingredients for success:

- *"She believed she could, and so she did!"*

- *"There is no elevator to success; you must take the stairs."*

- *"Success is the result of perfection, hard work, learning from failure, loyalty, and persistence."*[1]

There is some truth to these messages. Success is unlikely without hard work. But the emphasis on success being up to you and only you has a lopsided emphasis on the self.

If success is only a function of one person's hard work, then the person who worked hard should get all the credit when success happens. But as anyone who has succeeded in work, life, or relationships knows, there are other factors at play in our accomplishments. Rarely is an achievement the result of an individual's hard work alone; instead, it is usually the result of many people's efforts, including supporters, collaborators, cheerleaders, and vision casters, not to mention advantageous circumstances.

Success is never the result of the self alone, but of God's ability to do in and through us what we could not do by ourselves. For we know that "through [Christ] all things were made; without him nothing was made that has been made" (John 1:3), and that "from him, and through him, and to him are all things" (Rom. 11:36). The "all things" to which these verses refer include our success at work. Instead of running with the idea that our hustle and hard work will save the day, it may be better to say, "She believed she couldn't and so (God) did!"[2]

## SUCCESS: THE WORK OF GOD

For the Christian, success depends on the work of God. Did you see that in the Scripture above? *All* things were made through Christ. Everything we have, see, use, and enjoy is a result of Christ working in our world. We are all instruments and conduits of the Divine Designer. We are vessels through which the power of God is at work in the world. And yet when we do well at work—when we get a positive performance appraisal, when we win the contract, when our project is selected to move forward, when our artwork is commissioned, when our students score well—it is easy to reflect on our own skills and talents in the success and forget to give credit to God.

This tendency is both so common and problematic, God warned the Israelites about it as they were preparing to enter the Promised Land:

> "Be careful that you do not forget the LORD your God, failing to observe his commands, his laws and his decrees that I am giving you this day. Otherwise, when you eat and are satisfied, when you build fine houses and settle down, and when your herds and flocks grow large and your silver and gold increase and all you have is multiplied, then your heart will become proud and you will forget the LORD your God, who brought you out of Egypt, out of the land of slavery." (Deut. 8:11–17)

Scripture reminds us that God is the source of everything good, and it warns us against the sin of pride, against forgetting the Lord in the midst of success.

The ways we are gifted, the experiences we go through, and the skills we develop along the way are all a reflection of God's generosity. God gave you the abilities, opportunities, and even the gumption you have to work. God placed the people with whom you work and the responsibilities you have in your life there on purpose. Your work and your success are not merely a result of your hard-won efforts. Everything we have. Everything we are. Everything in our lives. It *all* comes from Christ. That means our breath, our minds, our strength, our abilities to do our jobs well, and the projects and tasks we complete—they are *all* the result of God working in you, through you, and for you.

## RESPONDING TO SUCCESS

So, what should we do in response to success? What is the proper and reverent reaction to God's actions in and through us? First, we give thanks. Over and over and over, the Scriptures model this attitude for us: Give thanks, for the Lord's love endures forever. Give thanks, for the good things God has done. Give thanks, for God's presence is with us. Give thanks, for all good gifts come down from the Father. Give thanks, give thanks, give thanks (Pss. 106, 107, 118, 136; James 1:17).

In the act of giving thanks, we express our gratitude outwardly—consciously affirming God's blessings and others' contributions to our lives. Doing this can help us to avoid hubris and instead develop appropriate humility. By acknowledging that we are not the masters of our own fate, and that the blessings in our lives have come as a result of grace, we take a stance against pride and push back the lie that we alone are responsible for the many good things found in and around our lives.

Fully living into the roles and responsibilities we have outside of work is another antidote to the pride and hubris that success can breed. Many high-powered and accomplished professionals also have to soothe babies in the night, drive in the school carpool, and help their kids with homework at the end of the day. Technology executive Sheryl Sandberg humorously describes having to call her husband, who was out of town, to find out what her kids needed in their school lunches, since he was the one who normally packed them.[3] As Al Erisman, former Boeing executive, said after a successful overseas conference where he was cheered for his contributions to the conference community, "When I get home, I will still have to take out the garbage."[4]

## GRATITUDE AND SERVICE

Your work is meant to serve others. God purposed it for good. It is meant to elevate and display integrity, creativity, and innovation, and to contribute to flourishing around the world—all of which ultimately point toward the attributes of God. Your work is intended to bring out the best in others, not just in yourself. In a cutthroat competitive environment, remembering the importance of serving others can change the narrative of your work. It is not just about reaching a goal, pleasing a boss, or making the company a lot of money. Neither is your work about showcasing your talent, demonstrating how much better you are than your competitor, or beating out the next person for the sale. Your work was designed to make life better for those who cannot make it better for themselves. You are a conduit, a vessel, an instrument through which God's power flows in your particular corner of the world. Let that sink in for a minute. Your work is not about you! So when success comes your way, it is not about you either.[5]

Serving others through our work is a way we can turn the temptation toward hubris into an expression of humility and gratitude. The life of Joseph in the book of Genesis is an example of this choice. After years of imprisonment for a crime he did not commit, Joseph's promotion by Pharaoh could have resulted in bitterness and the desire to take revenge on those who had mistreated him (Gen. 41). In a position of power, at the right hand of the king, Joseph may have been tempted to make the position self-serving. After all, he was the second most powerful man in all of Egypt! Instead, Joseph dealt with his reversal of fortune as a grounding event—one through which he expressed gratitude and humility, choosing to serve those whom he could have easily commanded. Being grounded in the ordinary tasks of life, sticking with his family, and remaining connected to God (through gratitude) were all ways in which Joseph took the high road and allowed his promotion to be an opportunity for service—and he ended up saving the lives of his entire family as well as countless others.[6] In fact, he named his two sons after what *God* had done, not after his own abilities and power (Gen. 41:51–52).

Recognizing that our successes are not our own is a perspective that challenges our broken humanity and our cultural norms. Humility and an intentional focus on elevating others are not natural attitudes and demeanors with which we arrive at work each day, but rather the result of God's Spirit living in us. The Holy Spirit shapes our hearts toward the service of others and uses our work to build others up. When our lives are controlled by the Spirit, we display the fruit of the Spirit: love, joy, peace, patience, kindness, goodness, faithfulness, gentleness, and self-control (Gal. 5:22). These virtues are not the result of our hard work or effort, our persistence or grit. Rather they are *a gift*, given freely out of the Father's radically lavish love toward his sons and daughters.

## PRACTICING GRATITUDE

As we explained in the introduction, engaging in any practice will not necessarily bring about a change. The practice is not what changes our hearts. It is the Holy Spirit's work *through* the practice that produces in us what we could not produce on our own. Gratitude opens us to the possibility of God changing us. It is the entry point through which humility and a proper perspective about life can grow, allowing us to experience joy when we give up exclusive rights to our success.

Accomplishments and success at work can be impetus for two types of gratitude: expressing our thanks for others and expressing our thanks to God. First, we can acknowledge the contributions of those whose guidance, input, contributions, and efforts contributed to the achievement. When success comes to us or our unit or organization, instead of reflecting on how much better we are than the next person or team or company, we can publicly and privately thank and recognize those who contributed to the success. This is especially important for those who may not normally receive recognition.

Second, we can become aware of and express gratitude for the opportunities we have had to be the conduits of God's grace, love, and mercy in the world. Rather than reflecting on the role we had in the success, we can focus on the impact the success may have had on others and in accomplishing God's purposes in the world. The medical professional can thank God for the opportunity to join with God in healing. The legal professional can thank God for the opportunity to promote justice. The businessperson can thank God for the opportunity to provide goods and services that contribute to human flourishing. The machinist can thank God for the opportunity to build something that will improve others' lives. The parent can thank God for the opportunity to contribute to the intellectual, social, and moral development of their children. Whatever your role, as you become increasingly aware of the ways you are serving through your work, you can in turn celebrate God's work through you.

When the sale is made, give thanks. When the student finally gets it, give thanks. When the software ships, give thanks. When the goods are delivered on time and in good condition, give thanks. When you are able to provide the care a patient needs to feel better, give thanks. When you come to the end of your rope and unexpectedly find you have more to give to the child or parent in your care, give thanks. When the business grows and is able to serve a larger customer base, give thanks. When you come up with an idea, give thanks. When the sentence is written well and describes the event precisely, give thanks. In everything, give thanks.

## THE EFFECTS OF GRATITUDE

Scripture reminds us to give thanks, and so we should—regardless of the outcome. But there may be some practical effects of giving thanks as well. An increasing body of research demonstrates so many positive impacts of gratitude that the findings sound almost like an infomercial for a miracle drug! In a number of studies, people have been asked to keep a "gratitude journal," where they list things at the end of each day or week for which they are thankful. Those who keep these journals experience a number of psychological benefits. They experience more positive emotions throughout the day and report higher levels of happiness than those who did not engage in the practice.[7] Those who keep gratitude journals also experience physical benefits: These people sleep better[8] and have better mental and physical health[9] than those who do not document the things for which they are thankful.

Other research has found that people who express gratitude are more likely to develop friendships,[10] to experience empathy toward others,[11] and to have resilience in the face of failure. God knows it is good for our souls to remain grounded in the reality that there are other people and circumstances at work besides just our own. And we reap the benefits when we make an effort to identify and call out those things for which we are thankful.

Recognizing that we have much for which to be grateful changes us, and when we express our gratitude it changes others. In fact, we often misjudge the impact of saying "thank you."

A recent study showed that people significantly underestimated the surprise and joy a thank-you note actually generated. In other words, expressing our thanks to others has more of an impact than we may think.[12] This should be all the more reason to give thanks. Speak thanks, write thanks, and pray thanks to the One from whom all blessings flow.

## CELEBRATING SUCCESS

Giving thanks is one way to handle success with humility. Another way to react is to celebrate! Celebration could be viewed as a self-serving opportunity for self-congratulatory remarks after some achievement. But it does not have to be this way. In Scripture, we see regular calls to celebrate. In the Old Testament, we see examples of feast days and days of celebration built into the Jewish calendar. These were holidays that served as regular reminders that good things come from God—not the equivalent of award ceremonies that recognize those who did well, but rather parties celebrating what God had done among the community.

These Jewish celebrations are opportunities to gather in community, enjoy good food and drink, and play. Many of those who follow God closely are the ones who put on feasts in celebration of God's goodness. In the book of Genesis, we see Abraham hosting feasts celebrating various family milestones. Isaac, David, Jonathan, the disciples, the early church, and even Jesus hosted meals and parties, celebrating the goodness of God. These are not low-key celebrations. The Jews really know how to celebrate! As Christians, we have our Thanksgiving, Christmas, and Easter celebrations, which last multiple days and all center on the worship of God, recognizing God's goodness, presence, and activity among the people. Imagine singing, dancing, feasting, bringing good tidings, and most of all thanking God.

## CELEBRATION THROUGH OFFERING

These Old Testament feasts were opportunities to celebrate, but they also involved sacrifices. Killing the fattened calf, the sacrificial lamb, a goat, or a dove as an offering to God was customary during this time. This notion of sacrificing an animal seems odd to us who have not been raised in such a culture. And while these sacrifices had a theological purpose that is no longer necessary since Jesus provided himself as the ultimate sacrifice, there is another aspect to them that may still fit our modern sensibilities. When the Jews offered sacrifices, it was a tangible way of recognizing and responding to God's blessings in their community, a way of giving thanks. This kind of offering does make sense to us, and there are ways that some churches today give congregants opportunities to make offerings of their work to God.

John Knox Presbyterian Church in Seattle had people bring a physical representation of their work to a Thanksgiving service. People brought keys, flash drives, projects, and paperwork that represented their work life and physically laid them on the altar in the front of the sanctuary. For the congregants, laying these items before God was a physical representation of offering their work activity to God, and it was also a way of acknowledging that success in the realm of work is accomplished only through God's goodness.

## CELEBRATION IN THE WORKPLACE

In church, celebrating the goodness of God is welcomed and even commanded, but how can we carry these same experiences and practices into our places of work? Many of us work in settings where God is not publicly acknowledged, so how can we appropriately express gratitude and celebration in these places?

First, we can take time regularly to identify what is going well on a team. Instead of jumping into meetings or brainstorming sessions with the tasks at hand, take some time on a regular basis to affirm your team members, their contributions, and their work. People do not hear "thank you," "great work," or "I really appreciated when you . . ." often enough. By taking time to show our appreciation, especially publicly, we practice gratitude for what has gone well at work. Even if you are not in a leadership position, acknowledging those you work alongside, and their work, can be a way of saying, "I see you, and I see that you're working hard."

Second, we can celebrate the completion of a project. When a project is finalized, the finished product is often not at all what we pictured when we began work on it. Especially when there were challenges to overcome and problems to solve, completing a project is a big deal! It could be a solo project—a book gets written, a presentation given, a lesson taught, a delivery made, or a marketing plan completed. Or it could be a team project—a restoration, a rebranding, a conference, a school-wide assessment, a park clean up, or a toy drive. Whatever it is, taking time out of your regular schedule to celebrate its completion is a way to honor those who contributed to it. Depending on your workplace, you may not be able to overtly recognize God's activity and presence. Nonetheless, in recognizing those who contributed creativity, organization, hard work, and effort, you are honoring the God in whose image each person was made. By taking time to celebrate, you acknowledge the goodness and provision of God.

Third, we can celebrate employees for their contributions. Particularly, when we find ourselves in positions of influence and authority, we have the opportunity and responsibility to create a culture of gratitude. When we are in leadership, we can regularly celebrate those who work with and for us. To whom much is given, much is required (Luke 12:48). Part of that requirement is being a good model for others by expressing your gratitude for their contribution and calling for a celebration for the good work accomplished.

Thanking those who work for you can be a huge morale booster. When we thank people for their work, we acknowledge that we could not do our work without them; we recognize their contributions to the larger whole. By thanking others, we thank God for them. By thanking others, we put into practice gratitude. By thanking others, we humbly acknowledge that our work is a way of serving others through employment, livelihood, and purpose.

Lastly, we can practice gratitude and celebrate God's goodness to us by giving credit to others for how they have helped a larger task succeed. There are times when credit is given to leaders for a task or project's success, when the leader actually did very little or had a small piece in a much larger endeavor. A store receives the "Most Profitable Award," a school receives increased test scores, a sports team wins a big competition, a company completely refurbishes a downtown area, or a department streamlines processes to make the company more productive. These are all instances where credit could be assigned to the wrong people, depending on the culture of the organization. If and when this happens to us—as the store manager, the principal, the coach, or the CEO—it is important to give credit to those who put in the long hours and hard work. Sometimes, we may be able to do this publicly. At other times, the best we can do is privately recognize those who contributed and thank them for their contribution. None of us succeeds on our own; by giving thanks, we give credit where credit is due.

Communicating ways we are grateful to others through notes of thanks, prayers of thanksgiving, or regular feedback can become an antidote to pride. While publicly attributing a team's success or completion of a project to God may not be possible in some work settings, we believe expressing gratitude and celebrating others are deeply spiritual practices that result in physical and mental health benefits, as well as shape work culture in profound ways.

## STORIES OF GRATITUDE AND CELEBRATION

### *Danica's Story*

Danica is a high school student who decided to be intentional about practicing gratitude in her life. She'd begun to recognize that she was quick to notice and reflect on what was not going well, but less likely to notice the positive elements of her life. Then a Christian teacher encouraged her to pay attention to the ways God may be speaking to her in everyday experiences. She then began looking for the positives, committing to keeping a gratitude journal each night. Some days it was hard to find at least one thing for which she was grateful or that had made her happy. Someone saying "hi" to her between classes made the list one day. Another day, it was going out to see a movie with friends. As she practiced gratitude, Danica decided she did not want to list the same thing twice. This expanded both the effort required to find something for which to be thankful, as well as her repertoire of gratitude.

Events she had previously glossed over when she began the practice became occurrences to write down; for as her gratitude list grew, so did her ability to see the goodness of God around her. Little by little, she began seeing a change in her attitude. She began to look for what she could write down at the end of the day. Sometimes she would be in the middle of an activity and have the sudden thought that this would be a great item to write down in her gratitude journal.

What Danica experienced in this practice was the expansive nature of gratitude to God. When we begin paying attention to the goodness of God all around us, it multiplies. As we see one thing for which to be grateful, we then wonder why we had been so upset the day before and if the event could be turned over and examined in a different light—the light of God's goodness. When we do this, our vision changes and we begin to see God's presence and activity in ways our pessimistic and cynical vision did not allow. Even as a high school student, Danica was able to find the power of God to bring light on those days when it seemed hard to find things for which to be grateful.

## Ross's Story

When Ross moved into a leadership position in his organization, he realized that there were very few "levers" he could utilize to reward people for their work. He did not have much control over the compensation, benefits, or promotion opportunities of his employees. But Ross realized that he could control how he interacted with those he led, and that these interactions could have a significant impact on the culture of his unit. He began to look for and acknowledge the efforts that others were making, regularly extending his thanks to them and their contributions to the organization's mission.

Ross found that recognizing his fellow employees through the act of gratitude highlighted the value of each person's contributions and became an antidote to resentment and pettiness. Saying "thank you" surfaced each member's giftedness and promoted a culture of celebration. Simply put, achieving the organization's mission required the good work of others, and sharing a heartfelt thank you to those who were engaged in this good work communicated his love, respect, and gratitude for them. Ross became known as a boss who recognized others, and this created a strong sense of affirmation and belonging within his division.

The practice of gratitude also became a discipline for Ross. As he expressed his thanks, he was reminded of the ways that he was dependent on others. Saying thank you impressed upon him that there were many tasks he did not do alone. Regularly recognizing the contributions of others reinforced in his own understanding of how much had been given to him. Each time he expressed his gratitude to his employees, it became a reminder of God's goodness and love to him.

## Al's Story

Al worked for many years leading the internal research and development group at an airplane manufacturing corporation. His group contributed services to a number of other divisions at the company, providing tools to help design and build airplanes. Al wanted to recognize the people in his group for their hard work and looked for ways to do that. They considered having a celebratory party at an expensive resort where individuals' contributions could be publicly acknowledged and cheered, similar to the way the sales group acknowledged its best salespeople. But the researchers in R&D did not seem to be motivated by this type of celebration. Instead, these employees seemed to find gratification in knowing that their work was appreciated by the larger company and that they made a difference in the development of its airplanes.

Instead of an annual party, Al decided to acknowledge key accomplishments of the employees in his group by recognizing how their particular work had an impact on something bigger. A poster of a new airplane was posted in the coffee room with the names of people and the work they did highlighted on the picture. Dave had developed the geometry, allowing the design of the faring between the wing and the body. Jim had contributed to the propulsion system. Evin's work in flight path optimization was an important part of the success of the airplane, so her work was placed near the avionics.

The celebration of the work of the employees in the R&D group became an ongoing theme rather than a one-time event. Anyone walking through the building would see pictures and examples of the work of the individuals in the group. This recognition and celebration became a big part of why people loved to work in the group.

## THE PRACTICE OF GRATITUDE AND CELEBRATION

The practice of gratitude and celebration does not have to be lavish and time consuming. The more you practice gratitude, the more grateful you will become. As we saw in Danica's story, gratitude begets gratitude; and celebrating people's efforts, whether a project succeeded or not, is a way to bring the goodness of God into the workplace.

You can enter into this practice by intentionally setting aside time on a consistent basis to give thanks to those around you, and to God who has empowered the work being done in your workplace. Think back to the beginning of the book when you wrote out your work rhythm. For some, there are natural breaks and deadlines where you do certain tasks or complete certain endeavors. For the teacher or professor, there are breaks between terms. For those in business, there is the end of a fiscal year or the end of the fiscal quarter. For those who are janitorial professionals, there are short- and long-term projects to keep the building's maintenance in order. For medical and emergency professionals, there are ends of shifts and ends of a stretch of multiple-day shifts. Each of these can be natural times to pause and consider how you might give thanks and celebrate.

Whatever your natural work rhythms, find spaces where being intentional about giving thanks—in large and small ways—fits into your work rhythms. Then take some time to enter into some of these practical ways to give thanks, express gratitude, and celebrate those around you. Here are some ideas:

- Make a list of five things for which you are grateful at work. Enter into a conversation with God about how you can go about giving thanks and celebrating those things, tangibly. Then go and do it!

- Make a list of three people who have had a positive impact on your work or your career. Send each of them a thank-you card expressing your gratitude for them and how they have supported, helped, or cheered you on in your working life.

- List ways you can celebrate your gratitude. It may be taking a group of people out to lunch, planning a day out of the office to be together, buying a gift, or recognizing them in a public setting. Then take your list and choose a few things to do. Make a plan for how you will intentionally give thanks for those who have contributed to your life. These celebrations might not occur on a daily or even weekly basis, but whatever the frequency, acknowledging others can remind you to be thankful for how the Lord has been at work in your work.

- Another way to do this on an ongoing basis, at the end of each week, is to identify a small handful of specific occurrences during the week for which you were thankful. Recognize God's goodness and presence on that interaction, project, or activity. Then do something tangible to acknowledge the people involved.

Remember that gratitude begets gratitude, so the more you practice this, the more you will find yourself grateful for many things—and people!—in your work.

## QUESTIONS FOR REFLECTION OR DISCUSSION

1. *Have you ever been in a workplace where your contributions did not seem valued or celebrated? Where no one said thank you for what you were doing? How did that impact your attitude or your work outcomes?*

2. *Have you been in a workplace situation where gratitude toward your work was regularly expressed and your contributions were celebrated? What was the impact of this experience on your work? On the rest of your life?*

3. *After reading this chapter, which of the ideas presented are practices you would like to incorporate into your working life? Where in your work rhythm will you incorporate them? How?*

4. *How did practicing gratitude and celebration go? What did you notice about your relationship with God as a result? What impact did the practice have on those with whom you work? What impact did the practice have on you (your thoughts, attitudes, or actions)?*

# 7

# CONFESSION AT WORK

He was the highest ranking official in his country and had everything at his disposal—wealth, military forces, commanders, and advisors who would respond to his beck and call. In addition to having political and military power, he was charismatic, attractive, and sensitive. Women flocked to him, eager to get close and do his bidding. He had faith in God and was confident that the Lord had specially appointed him to his position of power and authority.

To most of those around him, his life appeared totally put together. He had everything. And yet—as all of humanity has found since Adam and Eve's experience in the garden—it was not enough. There was one thing just out of his reach: her. Another man's wife. He could see her from his window and watched her as she bathed on the roof of her home, the home of one of his commanders. He knew her husband was away due to his command responsibilities. Perhaps because she was just out of reach, David found her more desirable than ever.

Bathsheba was her name. He had her brought to his palace and then slept with her—she was in no position to reject the advances of the king. What he should not have had now become his. But— as Adam and Eve also found out—there are consequences when our lust drives our decisions. Obtaining what is just out of reach is never as satisfying as it seems it will be; and when the consequences hit home, it becomes clear that what was truly needed was not the object of desire, but rather self-control, sacrifice, and contentment in what God has for us.

The weeks went by and David learned that Bathsheba was carrying his child. He knew he had to contain the scandal before it grew. Her husband, Uriah the Hittite, could not find out. But when David's plans for a cover-up went awry, he sent Uriah to the front lines, along with a secret message to his general that Uriah—one of David's top commanders—should never come home. And so, Bathsheba's husband was killed in battle and she gave birth to the king's son. Life could never be the same after that. David had compromised her whole family as well as his own position of moral leadership, and they all reaped the consequences of his behavior: inner turmoil, relational strife, and the death of the son.

When David royally messed up, he at first tried to avoid the consequences of his actions, but this ended up creating an even more disastrous outcome. Eventually, the prophet Nathan confronts him; and instead of hiding from the truth, David confessed and acknowledged his responsibility for what had happened. David went to God and repented. He recognized that he had been seduced by the power and prestige of his position. His own lusts got the better of him, and he had to take responsibility for the result. As much relational turmoil as he had caused, even more seriously, he created a rift with his God, the one who had appointed him to his position of power in the first place.[1]

"Cleanse me, clean me, restore me," David begged God in Psalm 51. He confessed; he told the truth about what he had done. He told the truth of his lust and the result of it. He came clean. This was a turning point for David. He could have tried to hide from God. He could have brushed his behavior under the rug, turned his back on the friend who confronted him about his actions, and decided that since he was king the rules did not apply. But his relationship with God was so vital that instead he chose the way of confession and truth-telling. He then appealed to God's mercy and grace, asking God not to cast him away and to restore the joy of his relationship with the Lord.

David made a huge mistake and then compounded it, putting the course of his rule at risk. But in the midst of it all, through confession, he also taught us the ways of restoration and repentance and lives out the call to truth-telling and truth-living. Confession in relationships, work, and our vocations is a central practice to being a disciple in the workplace.

## OTHER CONFESSION IN SCRIPTURE

While Adam and Eve's disobedience in the garden brought severe consequences, acknowledging their betrayal brought God's grace and goodness upon them. This mercy may seem severe at the time, but it is exactly what is needed for us to become who God desires us to be.

When we refuse to confess, we stray even more into the shadows of sin and brokenness in our work and in our relationships. In the Old Testament, Cain's unwillingness to take responsibility for his anger resulted in his murder of his brother. David's initial act of adultery snowballed into lying and murder as he attempted to cover up what he had done. As we observe in both of their cases, anger, pride, and fear prevent people from confessing. Through Moses, God gives the Hebrew people the Ten Commandments as a way of keeping them from that which will damage their relationships with one another and with their God. Not only does God give them the law, but he also provides them with a way to confess that brings them back into relationship with him. The Levitical law was instituted as a way to tell the truth about the ways in which they had fallen short and sinned against God.

Prior to the Levitical law, there was no systematic way for the people of God to acknowledge and come clean from their sin. But when God gave Moses the commandments that would become the moral and ritual guides for the Hebrew people, God also provided a system for active and regular repentance and sacrifice. Built into the rhythm of Israelite life was a new way of confession, one with physical manifestations as well as spiritual. The need for regular sacrifices and offerings was difficult, cumbersome, and costly. The path that God created required work—hard work—for the people to be freed of their sin. This way toward reconciliation required the Israelites to acknowledge the truth of their own complicity.

As we know from the Scriptures, this detailed system of repentance and forgiveness through ritual sacrifice was not easy. There was work to be done to bring the truth into the open. Like the Hebrews, we too know that bringing the truth into the light and exposing our true selves can be difficult. Instead of confessing, we can be tempted to play the blame game as Adam did with Eve and as Eve did with the serpent. It is easy to be angry with others for the roles and responsibilities we believe they have in our own behaviors. We may not want to acknowledge that we are the kind of person who would sin *that* way. We also may be afraid of what others will think if they find out: What could be the implications for our relationships? For our reputation? For our career? These fears tempt us to stay in the dark, hiding what we have done at all costs.

But confession—telling the truth about ourselves and what we have done—moves us back into the light. Stepping out of the shadows, we find that confession not only shines the light on the truth, but it also brings the light of God's forgiveness and love straight to us. Through confession, we admit our responsibility and move toward the possibility of reconciliation with God and with others.

## CONFESSION FOR HUMILITY'S SAKE

Most of us do not like to acknowledge our mistakes and wrongdoing. Our resistance to confession seems to be built in to the fallen human condition. When my (Denise) children were small, my husband and I used sign language to communicate with them. One child in particular developed a significant signing vocabulary, using about sixty signs by the time he was a year and a half old. Typically, when teaching a word we would model its sign, say it out loud, and then shape his hands into the same form. This worked well for all the signs except one. When we tried to teach him "sorry," he actively resisted our efforts to move his hand in the way that would convey the word. Even as a toddler, he did not want to communicate that he was in the wrong. Perhaps this should not have been a surprise!

Confession requires honesty with ourselves and humility before others. As a result, confession is quite uncommon and often difficult for most people. We do not see it modeled by others very often, and it may be even less common among people with higher levels of responsibility and authority. And yet, confession is *the tool* God uses over and over again to grow us, to shape our character, and to make us into the likeness of Christ. Confession can lift a heavy burden, enable us to start anew, and remind us that God's mercies truly are new every morning.

Confession, however, is not a magic elixir that removes the consequences of our actions. As we saw in the story of David and Bathsheba—and as you may know from your own life—sin has consequences that confession does not eliminate. At its heart, confession is truth-telling. It requires us to be honest about the ways we have not measured up and to admit the hurt that we have inflicted on others and on our Creator. This is what makes confession so difficult: It requires us to face the deeply painful truths about ourselves. But it is only in facing them that we can move beyond them.

If confession were merely a tool to shape us and lift heavy burdens from our lives, then we would most likely jump at the chance to confess our wrong and be restored into relationship with those we have wronged. Who does not want a burden lifted? But, as anyone who has sinned knows, it is the consequences that we find ourselves running to avoid. We live in the shadow of Adam and Eve, hiding among the trees and not wanting to be found out. We have inherited the impulse to blame others for our own wrongdoing. We fear the experience of humiliation and shame and do everything we can to protect ourselves—almost at all costs.

We do not want to be fired, reprimanded, or written up; we do not want to know the true state of our souls and the effects of our sin-infested hearts; and so we do everything we can to avoid having the truth come to light. This happens especially in the workplace, with those with whom we come into closest contact.

When we do not fess up to the ways in which we contributed to what went wrong, our work becomes something to hide behind, rather than something in which we are shaped and used by God. Our purpose for working gets twisted in a tradition as old as humanity. Instead of work being about joining in with what God is doing in the world, without confession it becomes about us and what we are accomplishing. Work, which at our best moments we recognize as a vehicle for God's activity in the world, turns into a place where we hide from God. The more we guard our own worth, power, and prestige, the less we are likely to confess the places where we have contributed to the brokenness of our work.

Confession is something of a paradox. We want to avoid it because of its potential to expose our weaknesses and flaws. But when we have the courage to enter into its embrace, it becomes a gift, allowing God to transform and use us.

As we already mentioned, this does not mean that the consequences of our actions are eliminated through confession. At times, these consequences may be severe. This is the nature of sin. But the gift of confession is that *truth-telling always frees us*. In confession we step out of hiding in Adam's shadow and into the light of God's loving kindness and grace. Telling the truth may bring with it a whole gamut of circumstances through which we would rather not put ourselves, not to mention those close to us who may also suffer from the consequences. Confession, however, also brings with it the freedom of truth. In this freedom, we can trust that none of the circumstances in our lives are wasted—*everything* can be used to shape and form us for God's good purposes.

## FREEDOM THROUGH CONFESSION

In John 8:31–40, Jesus tells those who have never been in forced slavery that "the truth will set you free." They dispute this. They were never slaves, so how could they be freed? But Jesus says plainly that it is sin that traps people into slavery. Sin makes you a slave. As we saw with Adam and Eve, as well as with David, sometimes something that is just outside of our reach is also something that can seem so enticing, capturing our time and attention as we become slaves to our desire. Our desires then dictate where we go and what we do.

The *truth* is what sets Jesus' disciples free. It is also how we find ourselves back in God's embrace. Telling the truth about who we are, what we have done, and the ways we have hurt others *is* the path to freedom. When we tell God and others about the ways in which we have become tangled up in sin, sin loses its grip on us. When we tell the truth, it becomes the key that unlocks the chains of lust, covetousness, jealousy, and pride that bind our lives. Like a python that suddenly discovers a different prey and lets go of whatever it is wrapped around, so confession loosens the grip that sin has on us.

To be clear, there is a distinction between confessing unintentional mistakes and confessing moral errors. Unintentional mistakes may include miscommunication, forgotten tasks, or an error in a report. Even when unintentional, these mistakes can hurt our coworkers, hold up projects, and cause frustration in the work environment. But unintentional mistakes are different from the choices we make that we know are wrong. Often the effects are different, the personal consequences are different, and how we grow from them is different. Moral errors are intentional and typically have more far-reaching impacts. They implicate the heart in ways that mistakes do not.

While there is a distinction between the two, both may require confession. When we are in the wrong—whether intentionally or not—confession is required. In confession, we tell the truth, opening the way to making amends and working through the issues in a way that brings freedom, restitution, and ultimately reconciliation to those involved.

Of course, sometimes the truth hurts—badly. Consequences ensue. We must live with the results of our actions, certainly. But freedom has always come at a price.

## CONFESSION IS COUNTERCULTURAL

As we have seen, while we might be tempted to run away from confession, especially in the workplace, turning toward confession can benefit us individually as well as our organizations. But it does not come naturally. Confession is extremely countercultural—perhaps today more than ever. Turn on any television channel or scan any news site, and you will see how our culture has deteriorated into a society-wide argument of he said/she said. Evidence points in every direction and allegations of "fake news" are lobbed at and by both sides of too many conflicts. Instead of people embracing humility, we see defensiveness and divisiveness. The majority of our business and political leaders seem to be oriented toward protecting their positions at all costs, rather than seeking after the truth or doing what is best for others.

Shortly after becoming the leader of a large manufacturing company, the new CEO was surprised to find during the weekly leadership meetings he held with the heads of the company's various plants that each one shared how their business goals were on track.[2] Using a green, yellow, and red color scheme to identify potential problems, all 320 status charts representing the company's progress toward its goals were green. Finally, after a few weeks of this, in exasperation the CEO said, "You know in the last year we lost $14.7 billion. Is there anything that is not going well?" This was a turning point for the company. The next week, one of the division heads showed a red for one of his goals. The room got very quiet, and heads turned to see how the CEO would respond. The CEO cheered the report—not because the goal was not being met, but because the truth was on the table. And once the truth was told, there was the possibility of addressing the problems underlying production. This is the power of humility in confession. Telling the truth takes courage, but it can also lead a team or an organization toward better partnership and ownership of their work.

Confession requires humility, a desire for the truth, and a willingness to make amends when we are in the wrong. It is a recognition that the ways we have been doing things may not be in the best interest of everyone involved. This type of confession invites the listeners into a redemptive dialog about what healing and reconciliation might look like. It also brings with it the willingness to change, learn, and find new ways of being in the world. Through confession, we invite and receive a renewed hope.

Since confession is a way that God responds to our lives with mercy and grace, when we participate in the practice of confession with wisdom and humility, this breathes freshness into our work that many people rarely experience. God's presence is ushered in when we tell the truth, whether or not God's presence is acknowledged in the workplace. Regardless of a person's level in the organization, whether a leader or an entry-level employee, the act of publicly stating that we were wrong and discussing what we will do to make restitution takes courage and humility. Confession is practiced when we tell the whole truth to those we have hurt—when we tell those who were counting on us that we failed. In turn, we find that we are actually braver and more apt to grow into a person of integrity than we may have originally thought. Truth-telling takes character and integrity to see ourselves as we really are, but *not stuck* as we are. Confession by its very nature shows those around us that, while we are human, we desire to be different. By telling the truth in confession, we grow more into the people God wants us to be.

In confessing where we fall short at work, we not only open the door for freedom to reign, but we also allow God to transform our work as we are molded and shaped as Christian workers. It is in this practice that we are ushered into the reality of God's mercy—a mercy that may at times be accompanied by severe consequences—but mercy nonetheless.

So, what would it be like to be people who are truth-tellers? Who have the humility to confess in the workplace? How might our workplaces change if we were to set this example at work?

## STORIES OF CONFESSION

### BJ's Story

BJ worked in a strategy role for a tech company where he was often privy to confidential information regarding strategic initiatives and potential acquisitions. Once after learning about an impending acquisition, BJ shared some confidential information with a friend. While BJ knew that sharing this was both illegal and unethical, he justified the decision in his own mind as helping out his friend. This friend used BJ's "stock tip" to produce substantial financial gains in the stock market. In short, BJ was guilty of insider trading or securities fraud.

The Holy Spirit convicted BJ that what he had done was both sinful and illegal. He knew he would need to confess his behavior both privately to the Lord and with others in his life—his wife and his pastor, as well as his company and the legal authorities. BJ's illegal activities ultimately resulted in the loss of his job and reputation, a large monetary fine, a two-year prison sentence, and a "felon" tag that will follow him for the rest of his life.

But BJ's story does not end with the punishment. The Lord poured out his grace and mercy on BJ and his family during this season. Since then, he has used his public stumble as a way to share his testimony with others and point to how God walked with him throughout his ordeal, in spite of his own behaviors. BJ readily admits that he is a work in progress, but he has come to recognize how confession resulted in peace and hope. His courage to tell the truth had life-altering consequences, but it also allowed God to do what only God can do: use his moral failure to bring about hope and change for the many who hear his story.

## Mark's Story

Mark was the in-house CPA tax preparer at a family business. After his first year on the job, he noticed that his health care premium had increased. Rather than paying for it himself as his employment agreement specified, he allowed the company to absorb the $45 a month increase. This small decision compounded over time and through future premium increases. Four years later, Mark had embezzled over $7,000 from the business.

When the economy turned, Mark's position was eliminated. He left the company on good terms, with no one aware of what he had done. Mark even forgot about what he had done. Two weeks later, he e-mailed his boss to ask for a referral. She e-mailed back with a life-changing statement: "We found something wrong with your paycheck." Sick with worry and shame, Mark considered running away, turning to alcohol, or even suicide. Instead, he called his wife and told her that he had stolen money from his previous job. She could only ask "Why?"—to which Mark had no answer. How could he? He was a regular church attender and participated in weekly men's Bible studies; yet he had stolen money from a company where he had been a valued and trusted employee.

Although Mark knew he needed to confess his actions, the idea terrified him. His adult sons looked up to him. Would his family abandon him if they knew? What would his pastor and his friends from church think? Paying back what he had taken was the easy part. But Mark also knew he needed to acknowledge the truth of what he had done with clients, and that the consequences of his behavior would be serious. Mark decided to be honest. As a result, the State Licensing Board suspended his CPA license, and he and his family suffered bankruptcy and a short sale on their house.

In the months after his sin was exposed, Mark felt waves of shame at what he had done. But something surprising happened after he confessed to family members, friends, mentors, and colleagues: he experienced redemption. Through the process of confession, Mark began to believe the truth that Jesus had forgiven him, and he was able to accept that forgiveness for himself.

In the years since his career was upended, Mark has shared his story with business groups and with students. He now laughs when people say, "I thought you had it all together," recognizing that surface appearances are often misleading. As he was able to acknowledge his own weakness, he found that his relationships with his family and church community were strengthened. Now when he reflects on this chapter in his life, Mark says, "I know that Jesus cannot love me more. I am becoming fully healed in forgiving myself."

## THE PRACTICE OF CONFESSION

It might be tempting to say, "I've never done anything illegal or immoral at work, so I don't need to worry about confession." But most of the time, our confessional lives consist of less obvious and more mundane events. Take some time on a regular basis—daily or weekly—to ask the Holy Spirit to examine your heart and show you where you might have sinned at work. You might do this as a part of another practice (for example, the Prayer of Examen in chapter 10), or you might choose to engage in it as its own practice.

If the Holy Spirit brings something to mind, tell God the truth about what you have done. Name your sin before God. Use Psalm 51 as an example of confession. In this psalm, David confesses his sin with Bathsheba and asks for God's cleansing grace of forgiveness. You may want to use it as a structure for your own confession as well. Once you have confessed your sin to God, ask what else you may need to do. Do you need to speak a truth? Do you need to acknowledge a fault or failure to others? Do you need to apologize and request forgiveness from someone?

If you have done something that requires confession, then you may also need to apologize to those you have wronged. In order to be effective, your apology should be clear and specific about what you have done and what you are working to change in order to prevent a similar incident in the future.[3] Such an apology recognizes the harm that your words or actions have caused to someone else. For example, if you did not acknowledge the contributions of a colleague in a workplace presentation, you might say, "I'm sorry that I didn't talk about the role you played on the project. It was not right for me to make it sound as if I had done everything on my own. I'm sure you must have felt slighted that I didn't recognize your efforts, and I'm sorry I put you in that position."

Of course, confession may also lead to the need for making amends with or providing restitution to those you have wronged. What this will look like will depend on the circumstances of the offence. If you stole something, you may need to return or replace it. If you took credit for someone else's work, you may need to go back and tell others the truth of who did what.

And finally, a confession may also require you to ask forgiveness of others. Requesting forgiveness is not a common practice in our culture and may feel awkward. It also puts you at someone else's mercy. They may not want to forgive you, and you cannot force them to reconcile with you. All you can do is confess, make recompense, and ask for them for forgiveness.

## QUESTIONS FOR REFLECTION OR DISCUSSION

1. *Has anyone at work ever confessed something about their behavior or performance at work to you? Have you ever been in the wrong and confessed to someone at work? What was that like? What was the result?*

2. *After confessing to God, is it necessary to confess to people at work? Why or why not?*

3. *How would a confession be received in your particular workplace? Are there aspects of your work culture that would make it more or less likely to result in confession?*

4. *If you are a leader in your organization, how would you respond if someone who worked for you confessed a work-related wrongdoing?*

5. *Are there things you need to confess to God or others at work? What is God asking you to do?*

# 8

# LAMENTING WORK

When work is engaging, fulfilling, and meaningful, we find ourselves giving thanks (as we discussed in chapter 6). There are many redemptive, renewing, and rewarding aspects to work, and they should produce in us praise, gratitude, and celebration. In our own day when we experience fulfillment through our work, it is not typically because it is a restful endeavor that comes naturally with no exertion or difficulty. Rather, the best work experiences are those that require time and effort, energy and focus. Good work is good because it reflects some aspect of God's nature and intent at creation. Just as God paid attention to the details in the creation of the cosmos, so too our good work requires our attention, effort, and skill. Just as God saw that the work of his creation was good, we know that our work is good when it contributes to flourishing in the world or creates beauty, innovation, and order.

When we work hard, we experience God's pleasure in the *effort* we give to it and the *outcome* of the task. We enjoy the fruits of our labor after a project is completed, a lesson is taught, a patient cared for, or a goal is accomplished. The fact that work is hard does not by itself make it toilsome. The coalescence of our mind, heart, creativity, and effort toward some good end is likely challenging and perhaps difficult. But there is a difference between hard work and toil.

Anyone who has worked for very long knows that work is not always life-giving. There may be days or weeks or longer seasons of our working lives when boredom, difficulties, frustrations, fears, and broken relationships are our dominant experiences at work. Work has been marred by the Fall, and we now experience toil in our work lives. Although work was originally given as a gift, ever since Adam and Eve ate the forbidden fruit, it no longer fully reflects God's design. As with all of creation, work has been stained with the brutal reality of life outside of Eden.

## TOILSOME WORK

While work was meant to be productive, creative, and fulfilling, we know that the Fall changed all of that. In Genesis 3, God told Adam and Eve that the ground they worked will be cursed and their own work will be full of pain and toil (see Gen. 3:17). Although we often think of toil as difficult physical labor, the Hebrew word for it is broader than that. It might better be understood as "sorrow."[1] All work, whether physical or mental, has been impacted by the Fall. All tasks have aspects to them that create sorrow. While hard work was given as a gift at the creation, hard work *with toil* becomes difficult and sorrowful—work that does not result in much progress or joy.

In addition to the work itself being toilsome, the context in which work is undertaken is fallen, and the outcomes of the work are not always good. Adam and Eve were responsible for working the ground, for planting and harvesting food. When the ground became cursed, their work did not turn out the way they may have expected or hoped. The crops may not have grown as they were supposed to. Floods and famine lurked. Thorns and thistles sprouted where good seed was planted. Similarly, in our own work we may try to accomplish something, but it may not turn out the way we planned. Communication may not be received the way it was intended. Extra hours invested may not prevent the layoffs. Our best efforts may not result in the sale or the successful bid.

Finally, in the Genesis account, the Fall results in damage to people, to their relationships with one another and with God.

Adam and Eve no longer fully reflected the image of God. And as we saw in the last chapter about confession, Adam blamed Eve for his decision to eat the fruit, Eve blamed the serpent, and both of them hid from God. The damage to people that began after this has continued to plague humanity through the ages, seeping into our workplaces today. Our motivations to work are now separate from God's design. Lust for power and greed overshadows the promotion. Sin crouches at every corner, waiting to disrupt and dismantle once-healthy working relationships.

Recognizing the impacts of the Fall on our work can be helpful for us. We can see that there are some attitudes, behaviors, and ways of working that are in our control and some that are entirely out of our control, marred by the effects of sin. Among these include organizational systems that reward the self-aggrandizer, bosses who bully and demean, and inequities for racial and ethnic minorities and for women. A company may offer inadequate compensation for their workers, and those with the least power to change them are most affected. A fast-paced achievement-focused workplace may spin out of control, creating pressure and impossible trade-offs for those working there.

We may find ourselves in a workplace with a lopsided emphasis on performance outcomes and reap the consequences of unrealistic expectations. We can experience difficult coworkers whose agendas conflict with ours. Colleagues who were once friends may betray and undermine us in order to advance their own career goals. Our company may downsize, and we then experience job loss and unemployment. Or perhaps we are left overburdened with an unreasonable workload to compensate for those who have been let go. The possible scenarios are endless, and the impacts of the Fall in the workplace are as diverse as the people who work there.

A number of these workplace circumstances are outside of the control of any one person. Instead, they are the effects of systemic corrosion. Some circumstances may be caused by the choices and actions of someone else, but they are still outside of *your* control.

Whether it is the result of a broken system or the decisions of one or more individuals, finding yourself in a toilsome workplace situation that you cannot directly affect is worthy of lamenting in conversation with God.

## LAMENT: THE GIFT OF EXPRESSION

If experiencing the wonder of work produces in us celebration and gratitude, then how do we respond when work is less than ideal, frustrating, or even heartbreaking—with no end in sight? How do we as Christians address the systemic corrosion we come into contact with on a daily basis at work? How do we approach this experience of work with the redemptive imagination of Christ?

The book of Psalms provides Christian workers a model for expressing all of life's experiences and emotions. The Psalms are a compilation of everything we can say to God, including how we feel about our work. While we do find psalms of gratitude and celebration, we also find the psalmist lamenting to God about his life, his work, and his relationships. The lament is a type of prayer, lifted to God to express sorrow and heartbreak, particularly when we have limited ability to change the circumstances in which we find ourselves. To be clear, a lament is not a whine. Rather it is a prayer that opens us to God's response, input, and correction to the situation.

When we whine, we are merely trying to get something off our chests. A whine does not express a desire to change or a willingness to accept personal responsibility—either for the cause of the problem or for what our role might be in providing a solution. When we whine, we simply want someone to listen without responding. While there can be a time for this, whining is not the same as lament.

Lament produces change in us because it is a two-way *conversation* with God. There is humility in lament—an openness to listen and hear from God where we might have contributed to the sorrow of our circumstances. In lament, we listen for God's kind correction and wisdom for what the right response is to the situation that is out of our control. We lament when we speak to God and call out for help, acknowledging our own inability to repair what is broken. We lament when we tell the truth about the situation, but also leave room for attending to how God might lead us in it. It is a lament when all we can do is cry tears of frustration, knowing that our tears are enough for God's response. Sometimes our cries are the most honest thing we can do, and our Lord—who is close to the brokenhearted—rushes to console the faithful servant who is suffering.

When we lament, we invite God to be our *companion* in the sorrow and despair of our work, in the places where we are feeling miserable and stuck. Through lament, we invite *God with us* to our work, giving him the space to bring insight about where we may have contributed to the suffering. We also give God the space to do what only he can do—heal and bring newness and hope.

## SCRIPTURAL EXAMPLES

While we do not very often see or experience many examples of lament in the Western church today, when we look closely at Scripture, we see lament as one of the frequent ways people expressed themselves to God. Interestingly, many of these laments have to do with issues of vocation. They may be good models for us as we lament the toil in our own work.

### *Lament and Longing*

In 1 Samuel 1, Hannah laments to God about her inability to get pregnant. She longs for the vocation of motherhood and to have the opportunity to step into the societal position that mothers held in her culture. While Hannah's lament focuses on her infertility, it really encompasses the roles and responsibilities she longs to take on but which she has not had the opportunity to fulfill.

Have there been points in your working life where you longed to do something different, something more meaningful, something else you were passionate about, and yet found yourself stuck in a job, role, or relationship that was less than your heart's desire? If so, you are in good company with Hannah, who brought her hurt, heartache, and longing to God through lament.

## Lament and Calamity

Within the wisdom literature of the Old Testament, we have the seemingly tragic tale of Job.[2] At the beginning of the story, Job had everything—wealth, family, good health, and a position of leadership within his community—but he lost it all in crushingly quick succession. After they sit with him for seven days and seven nights, silently mourning with him "because they saw how great his suffering was" (2:13), Job's friends then begin to provide explanations for why he had experienced such misfortune—and to advise him on what to do next. Their "advice" ranges from telling him to be bitter, to repent of whatever he must have done wrong, to turn toward anger and whining, or to cling to the goodness that once was. His wife even says to him, "Are you still maintaining your integrity? Curse God and die!" (2:8). But Job rejects their explanations and advice and instead enters into lament *with God*. He expresses his deep heartache, sadness, and fears about what has been stripped away in his life, all the while leaving himself open to God's response in the conversation. If he had given into bitterness (or his wife's suggestion), it would have become a one-way conversation; but by entering into lament, he was able to listen to God's perspective, which was significantly different than his own, his wife's, or his friends. And when God finally spoke, Job could only respond with awe.

Have you been in a situation where you lost your health, people you loved, your position, or the influence you once held dear? Or maybe you're in a current season where there is loss all around you. If this is where you are, know that you are in good company. As it was for Job, lament may be a healing and helpful tool to use in interacting with God.

## Lament and Confusion

In the Gospel of John we find Mary and Martha, Jesus' confidants and faithful followers who have supported his ministry from the beginning. In John 11, we see that their beloved brother Lazarus is gravely ill. Having traveled with Jesus, the sisters have seen first-hand his power to heal and his power to restore life. And so they send word to him: "Lord, the one you love is sick" (John 11:3). But Jesus does not come right away. Although he does have the power to save Lazarus, he chooses to stay where he is for two more days. Oh, the agony Mary and Martha must have experienced over those couple of days, knowing there was someone who could act on their brother's behalf but who did not for some unknown reason—that is, unknown to them at that time.

Imagine what Mary and Martha may have been feeling when Jesus arrives on the scene. *You could have intervened and you didn't! If you had been here, he wouldn't have died!* Not only was their family torn apart with the loss of Lazarus, but Mary and Martha, as unmarried women in Jewish society, would also have lost their provider and source of economic security. Lazarus's death was both a loss of relationship and a loss of position for the sisters. It is a loss they contemplate in confusion—recognizing that they could have been saved from the situation *if only* Jesus had entered the home, put his hands on Lazarus and healed him.

Their lament comes in the form of confusion—confusion because of their faith in Jesus' ability to heal their brother. When he arrives, Martha is the first one to greet him. " 'Lord,' Martha said to Jesus, 'if you had been here, my brother would not have died. But I know that even now God will give you whatever you ask' " (11:21–22). Although she doesn't understand, she has unwavering faith in Jesus.

Then it is Mary's turn: "When Mary reached the place where Jesus was and saw him, she fell at his feet and said, 'Lord, if you had been here, my brother would not have died'" (11:32). Jesus was greatly moved by this time, and in John 11:35 we have one of the most amazing verses in all of Scripture: "Jesus wept." Here, God himself laments with his children.

Before Jesus does what the women can't begin to imagine he will do, he enters into their grief with them. This is no small act. Weeping with the women, we find Jesus to be the God who not only listens to our cries, but who also grieves with us—for all of our losses and confusion. While Mary and Martha could not predict the great miracle they were about to witness, their lament to Jesus is actually a sign of their faith. They trust Jesus with their anguish, not knowing that Jesus was about to raise Lazarus from the dead.

Although none of us have had the same experience as Mary and Martha in receiving their loved one literally back from the dead, we can certainly empathize with their confusion and grief. They did not understand why Jesus—who loved them and who loved Lazarus—would let their brother die when they knew he could heal him. Likewise, we suffer our own tragedies, not understanding why the Lord allowed this to happen to us.

Being fired from a job, being maligned by a coworker, going bankrupt, or having your possessions stolen can be painful—especially if you were not at fault, wondering why it happened this way. So too, having a vocational dream stripped from you due to illness, loss of employment or the death of a project, continued conflict with a coworker or boss, or changes to a job description can produce in us questions, grief, and discouragement.

Whatever grief you experience through your work is a lament God wants you to bring to him. Mary and Martha's lament to Jesus resonates with the confusion we experience when we know God can do something on our behalf and chooses not to, or when we sense God leading us in a certain direction only to find the way closed. God invites us to share the emotions we experience in these seasons and circumstances through prayers of lament.[3]

## STORIES OF LAMENT

### Steve's Story

Steve and his wife started building kitchen cabinets in their garage in the late 1970s. Over the next thirty years the company grew, moving to a large state-of-the-art factory and employing over two hundred people. Then the great recession of 2008 hit, and their world came crashing down. Nearly overnight revenues dropped by 60 percent and people had to be laid off. Within six months, the company had fewer than ninety employees and was running out of cash. Steve thought it was unlikely to survive.

As a faithful Christian, he wondered how this could be happening. His business had won awards, Steve was known as "Mr. Integrity," and he and his wife had been "so faithful" over all these years. One night in that dark summer, Steve spent an entire night on his knees crying out to God. Throughout the evening and the early morning hours, God peeled back the layers of Steve's self-sufficiency like the peeling of an onion. With every layer, the Lord seemed to say, "What are you so afraid of? Don't you trust me?" At about three o'clock that morning, Steve finally realized that his faith had been in himself and his own resources, not in God. He surrendered and said to God, "All right, it's all yours. Whatever journey you want me to go through, I will trust you to lead and direct my path—even if that means going through bankruptcy."

That time of lament for Steve was the beginning of a renewed commitment to trusting God's indwelling and provision for him and his family, regardless of the outcome. While the circumstances were beyond his control, he came to recognize that God was with him in the midst of the circumstances. God heard and took away his frustration and fear. The story of Steve's company has a happy ending (although not all laments do): A new product was launched in 2011 and took off like a rocket ship; today, the company is more than twice the size it was before the recession. However, if it had gone the other direction, Steve is confident that God would still be with him and that God's hand would be evident in his life. This is the power of lament. The gift we are given in lament is the companionship of God in the midst of whatever we are going through; and no matter where the circumstances take us, the gift is knowing God's presence and faithfulness wherever our lives lead.

## Gideon's Story

As a citizen of South Africa, Gideon worked for the Truth and Reconciliation Commission (TRC) in the late 1990s. The mandate of the commission was to investigate gross human rights violations that took place during the years of apartheid in South Africa. Gideon's work was very much behind the scenes: he sat in a booth with headphones and a microphone, doing simultaneous interpretation for people testifying before the commission. Sometimes the victims or survivors or experts gave their testimony, but typically Gideon's job entailed interpreting the testimony of the perpetrators. That meant that for about four days a week Gideon retold the stories, in the first person, of people confessing to abducting, torturing, and murdering other people.

During the two years prior to his work for the TRC, Gideon had fallen in love with the daily praying of the Psalms. When he began his translation work, telling the stories of horrific human rights violations, he found himself increasingly leaning on the Psalms—especially the psalms of lament. These psalms gave him a language for talking to God about what he was hearing and translating, a language of sorrow and rage. Many late nights when he was unable to sleep, Gideon talked with God through the psalms he read.

After two years of working with the TRC, Gideon described his prayer life as "narrowing down," focusing more on psalms of lament than any other type of prayer. And yet, in retrospect two decades later, he expresses gratitude "for this pittance of prayers, and in particular for Psalm 137, which—like a fetter—tethered my raging heart to the possibility of a just and loving God."

These prayers of lament gave voice to the heartbreak that Gideon suffered on a daily basis in his work. Because of the psalms of lament, he was given permission by God to pray with such passion, vigor, and rage. While our work won't always produce these types of prayers in our lives, because of the psalms of lament, we are given the freedom to express our intense emotional experiences to God—as a way of connecting, expressing, and healing.

## THE PRACTICE OF LAMENT

What would it look like for you to bring your current heartbreak or frustrations about work to God? They may be initially apparent to you, or they may be hidden in the recesses of your soul. If that's the case, think back to the examples of lament we've just seen from Scripture: Hannah, Job, and Mary and Martha. What resonated in these examples from Scripture for you?

Have you longed for a particular vocation, role, or responsibility but have only dreamed of it rather than living it? Have you been placed in a seemingly impossible position, and you're left wondering if you're up to the task? Has calamity struck your life or work, stripping away everything, like Job? Have you walked in one direction only to find the door closed or the project you poured your effort into shut down? If any of these pricked a place in your soul, then the practice of lament can be a starting place for opening up your frustration, heartache, and pain in conversation with God.

Where do I start, you might wonder? One way people have entered into the practice of lament is by writing their own psalms of lament. This practice involves taking a psalm of lament and personalizing it for your particular situation at work. You may find it helpful to take Psalm 12, 44, 54, or 86 and personalize it to your specific circumstances. For example, below on the left is a section

of Psalm 44. On the right is an example of how you could personalize this lament based on the death of a dream or an unwanted
redirection of vocation.

| Psalm 44 | Personalized Lament |
|---|---|
| 9 But now you have rejected and humbled us; you no longer go out with our armies. | *I feel rejected by you, humbled because I've lost control of my future and the direction I thought you were sending me in.* |
| 10 You made us retreat before the enemy, and our adversaries have plundered us. | *Why did you stop going before me and leading me? I have been attacked, ridiculed, and rejected!* |
| 11 You gave us up to be devoured like sheep and have scattered us among the nations. | *It feels as though my efforts were all for nothing, and now I wonder if you even care. Or are you far away, scattering my future this way and that? I feel like I* |
| 12 You sold your people for a pittance, gaining nothing from their sale. | *was a sold a false hope; why did you let me think this was where you were leading me?* |
| 13 You have made us a reproach to our neighbors, the scorn and derision of those around us. | *Now I look like a fool. All that hard work, all the commitment for nothing.* |
| 14 You have made us a byword among the nations; the peoples shake their heads at us. | *I walk into work and they whisper at me, wondering why I'm still there.* |
| 15 I live in disgrace all day long, and my face is covered with shame | *My days are so draining and I'm hurt!* *I feel taken advantage of and left out in the cold.* |
| 16 at the taunts of those who reproach and revile me, because of the enemy, who is bent on revenge. | *I'm ashamed and wonder what people are saying about me. I feel like the other shoe is going to drop soon.* |

17 All this came upon us,
   though we had not forgotten you;
   we had not been false to your
   covenant.
18 Our hearts had not turned back;
   our feet had not strayed from
   your path.
19 But you crushed us and made us a
   haunt for jackals;
   you covered us over with deep
   darkness.
20 If we had forgotten the name of
   our God
   or spread out our hands to a
   foreign god,
21 would not God have discovered it,
   since he knows the secrets of
   the heart?
22 Yet for your sake we face death all
   day long;
   we are considered as sheep to be
   slaughtered.
23 Awake, Lord! Why do you sleep?
   Rouse yourself! Do not reject us
   forever.
24 Why do you hide your face
   and forget our misery and
   oppression?
25 We are brought down to the dust;
   our bodies cling to the ground.
26 Rise up and help us;
   rescue us because of your unfailing love.

*Didn't I worship you? Wasn't my*
*work part of how I served you?*
*And now it's stripped away!*
*Didn't you have my heart, and*
*didn't I act with integrity?*

*And yet it seems like the darkness*
*of loss has swallowed me up!*

*You know the secrets of my heart.*
*The desires, the ways I've served.*
*It's all been before you, and yet*
*I'm not satisfied!*

*I feel like the death of this dream is*
*going to bring despair to my life*
*for a long time!*

*Do you hear me? Do you hear my*
*lament? I must hear back from*
*you! I must be brought back*
*into your presence. So, show*
*your face.*

*Please God, make sense of this!*
*Help me! Be close to me. Re-*
*member you promised unfailing*
*love, and I sure could use some*
*right now.*

This is just an example, but it may give you some starting points to write your own psalm of lament to God. Use one of the psalms as a guide but be as specific as you can to your situation. Remember that this is a conversation with God, not just a venting session to God. Leave time and space to listen to how God might respond to you.

What is the Lord saying to you about your role or responsibility in the situation? How might God be calling you to respond? Use these questions to enter into this practice of lament. You can use this practice on a regular basis, or you may choose to use it only in seasons of doubt or loss. No matter how you practice it, know that having a robust biblical spirituality includes expressing lament and inviting God to enter into conversation with you.

## QUESTIONS FOR REFLECTION OR DISCUSSION

1. *Are you more likely to try to find the positive in a given situation, or is it easier for you to lament what is broken? What are the advantages and disadvantages of your particular bent?*

2. *How would you describe the difference between whining and lament? Are you more prone to one or the other?*

3. *Have you experienced lament in your church setting? If not, why do you think that is?*

4. *Are there aspects of your work you should lament before God? Are you doing that? Why or why not?*

5. *Was the practice of writing your own psalm of lament helpful for you? Did you find it difficult? Why or why not?*

# PART THREE

# Reflecting On Work

Unless we pay attention to what God may be saying to us about our work, we cannot hope to hear God's voice in the daily and the mundane. We cannot change things of which we are not aware. Often, we go through our days and our work activities on autopilot. We know what to do, and we know the spoken and unspoken "rules" of our work culture. Yet without reflection, we may find ourselves stifled in our growth professionally, personally, or spiritually. Without time to reflect, we head down paths we never intended to go, because we didn't stop to realize where we are, whose we are, and what exactly we are called to do in our work.

Discerning the callings of our life doesn't begin with the big choices we have to make. Instead, when we come to know the voice of the Savior in the daily and seemingly insignificant aspects of life, hearing his voice in the major callings becomes easier. Reflection does just that. In reflecting on our work, we train the ears of our hearts to listen to the voice of God our shepherd, guiding us in the ways we are created to work and tuned to hear our deep identities in the midst of that work.

When we reflect, we are often convicted, redirected, and refined with respect to our attitudes and actions at work. Additionally, reflection enables us to pay attention to any insight God might have for us on relational dynamics, creative projects, problems to solve, or the motivations with which we approach our work.

Annie Dillard has famously said, "How we spend our days is of course how we spend our lives."[1] Without reflection, we don't realize how we are actually living out our days. Through reflection, God can bring clarity, peace, and a sense of direction for the Christian worker.

In this section, "Reflecting on Work," we explore three practices:

1. **Solitude: Alone in God's Presence.** *The practice of solitude, or taking time to be alone in the presence of God, can bring clarity to a working life that the other practices can't provide. This practice, when done for the purpose of focusing on co-creating with God, can be deeply formational, changing who you are and how you reengage with others in your work.*

2. **Prayer of Examen for Work.** *By deliberately reviewing your work day through guided questions, you invite the Holy Spirit to guide, correct, and speak into your working life. While there are a variety of questions people ask during an examen, this practice will introduce you to the concept of specifically asking questions about your work.*

3. **Sabbath: Ceasing from Work.** *By refraining from work one day a week, we open God's gift of rest. Practicing the Sabbath allows us space to reflect on the ways God is at work and the opportunity to engage in relationships with others.*

# 9

# SOLITUDE: ALONE IN GOD'S PRESENCE

He had been working many long, intense days when the news arrived: Jesus' cousin John, the one who had baptized him at the beginning of his ministry, had been beheaded. In drunken pride, King Herod had promised his stepdaughter anything she wanted, up to half his kingdom, after she danced for him at his birthday party. After conferring with her mother, Herodias (who had a personal grudge against John), the girl asked for John the Baptist's head on a platter. Not wanting to embarrass himself in front of his guests, Herod reluctantly agreed, and the head was brought to the girl (see Matt. 14 for the full account).

With his cousin dead, Jesus longed to get away, to be alone and pray. Jesus needed solitude and "withdrew by boat privately to a solitary place" (Matt. 13:14). But before the boat had docked, word spread that Jesus was coming and the people of that region showed up, bringing the injured, deformed, and sick to receive healing. Matthew writes that when Jesus "saw a large crowd, he had compassion on them and healed their sick" (Matt. 14:14).

The disciples must have sensed the fatigue. "This is a remote place, and it's already getting late," they said. "Send the crowds away, so they can go to the villages and buy themselves some food" (Matt. 14:15). They may have been thinking: *And then maybe we can get some time to ourselves—finally*! But Jesus, having compassion despite his fatigue, told the disciples that *they* could feed the crowd. The solitude they had sought was a dream—not today, not right now. Instead, Jesus chose instead to demonstrate God's power through another miracle—the feeding of five thousand people with only five loaves of bread and two fishes.

Jesus' own longing for solitude, though, had not been quenched. So, after they finished feeding the crowd, he sent his disciples away, knowing they too needed to rest. He told the disciples to go ahead of him to the other side of the Sea of Galilee. *I'll meet you, but you go ahead of me. I need rest. I need to be alone with my Father.* Then "he went up on a mountainside by himself to pray" (Matt. 14:23).

On that mountainside, Jesus was finally away from the cacophony of voices—children's laughter and adult discussions that had earlier filled the air. It was now quiet. He finally had what he longed for and had sought for many hours. Silence. Solitude. Time with the Father. Jesus remained in that place nearly all night, sharing intimacy with the Father. Perhaps he was lamenting the death of his cousin or seeking out the renewal of the Holy Spirit for what would come next in his work—or perhaps it was all of that.

What came next was yet another miracle. At four in the morning, having been filled by God during his time in solitude and prayer, Jesus walked on the water to his disciples, who were sailing in the boat to yet another location. What is important in this story is that Jesus had sought solitude for many hours before he actually experienced it. As we saw in this Gospel account, he had immediate work responsibilities that needed his attention before he could enjoy that solitude and silence. *But he never stopped pursuing it.*

For Jesus, solitude and prayer alone were integral to his work in ministry. The practice and what happened afterward are connected. However, it was not a magic practice where he could put in the time in solitude and get a miracle in return. Spiritual practices do not work that way! What is clear is the priority Jesus placed on the practice of solitude—and how important it was, especially when he was busy with his work.

## THREE KINDS OF SOLITUDE

While we have argued that bringing spiritual practices *into* the work setting can be transformative, the practice of solitude or taking time to be alone in the presence of God *outside* of work can also bring transformation to your work. Solitude is a classic spiritual practice dating back even before the time of Christ. There are many examples from the early church mothers and fathers going away to the desert or the monastery to hear from God. This practice has stood the test of time and continues to be helpful for Christian workers. Solitude can bring the rest, clarity, and connection we need to keep going forward in our work. Through times of solitude, we can be filled with God's purposes and renewed for our work in new ways.[1]

There are three types of solitude we see in Scripture that we can practice to deepen our connection with God and open ourselves to the power of the Holy Spirit in our work: (1) intentional time alone to listen to and commune with God; (2) intentional time alone to work in God's presence; and (3) involuntary times of solitude.

### Time Alone Listening to God

Taking a day, a half day, or a few hours of retreat to be alone with the purpose of reflection, prayer, and listening to God about one's work can be a highly formative practice for the Christian worker. This may be especially important for those whose work does not provide them with time by themselves. Every vocation has varying degrees of interpersonal relationships built in, and some jobs provide little opportunity for time alone. For example, medical professionals, caretakers, retail workers, teachers, stay-at-home parents, and those in service industries all experience the constancy of interactions with people in their work. So seeking solitude by taking time away from their regular responsibilities in order to pay attention to God's direction, accept the Lord's rest, and find refreshment in their work can provide the stamina they need to reenter those relationships.

For those used to being around people so much, experiencing solitude may prove to be difficult at first. When we habitually function at a high relational pace, it can drown out the sound of God's gentle but commanding voice in our lives. Regular times of solitude can provide a reset, changing the ways and the frequency of hearing from God. Part of the discipline of solitude is intentionally placing ourselves into a posture of listening. This can be hard to do in the middle of a job that demands our attention, and so taking time away from work to be with God is important. Becoming familiar with the voice of the Good Shepherd during times of solitude can tune your ears to hear this voice in the middle of the noise of relationships and everyday work.

Although solitude requires time away from regular workplace responsibilities, it does not necessarily require a long time away. You can look for short periods of time to be alone with God: reading scripture or praying while the toddler is asleep, taking a prayer walk during a break at work, or spending the last few moments in the car to be in the quiet presence of God before stepping out to go to work. There may, of course, be other seasons when opportunities for longer periods of solitude arise. Perhaps you can spend a day at a church retreat, or you have the chance to go on a personal retreat over a long weekend to seek God's guidance. You may be fortunate enough to be able to take a sabbatical where you have a few weeks or months away from your regular work. All of these can provide refreshment and renewal, allowing you to step away from the cacophony of your daily life and work in order to hear from the Lord.

Throughout Scripture, we see examples of people practicing solitude by spending time alone in silence, prayer, and intentional listening for God's voice. Moses, leader of the people of Israel, is called away to climb Mount Sinai by himself (see Exod. 20). He climbed the mountain and waited, and then God gave the Ten Commandments to him. God spoke clearly to him about how the relationship between the people and their Lord would work. For Moses, solitude was key to hearing God and learning how to lead.

The prophet Daniel learned the vocabulary of prayer, alone in the presence of God. This time by himself allowed him to recognize the voice of God, which enabled him to make his prayers public, leading by example in the foreign country of Babylon and then Persia. Regular and intentional solitude with God increased Daniel's faith, trust, and belief in God's power, which he was then able to demonstrate publicly and powerfully. Daniel's solitude with God developed in him the courage that propelled his work as a prophet.

Prior to the start of his ministry, Jesus was led by the Holy Spirit into the solitude of the desert. For forty days he was alone, and this time provided a significant catalyst to his ministry. It was in solitude that Jesus was tempted. During these days by himself, Jesus proved his trust in God, his ability to outwit Satan, and his confidence that the word of God is faithful and true.

## Working Alone in God's Presence

Spending intentional time to work alone in the presence of God is another way of practicing solitude. This can be time spent to specifically finish a project, write a proposal, or create an original piece of art, writing, or work. It can also be time to put together a financial report, plan an event, or clean a building. When you do any type of work alone, that process can be transformed into the practice of solitude. Being alone is not the key to this practice; many jobs have elements that are done solitarily. Just because you are working alone does not necessarily mean you are practicing solitude.

What is key is your mindset and intention in doing the work. As you work, are you listening for how God might direct, speak into, or shape the work you are doing? Are you acknowledging God's actions in and through you as you work? Does this awareness change what you are doing, how you are doing it, or the final product of your work? Is your work a divine conversation with God, rather than a frenzied race to finish the work and simply be done?

When work in solitude is done with a focus on co-creating with God—whether it involves creating a physical product, an intellectual report, or tending to something worth tending—working alone in the presence of God can change us and others. For example, an artist may be able to listen in different ways to the Holy Spirit's prompting to his artwork when alone than when he is surrounded by others in a noisy studio. The accountant may find the pleasure of God as she works to file and create a tax return in God's presence. The housekeeper may find connection with the Holy Spirit as she cleans toilets, vacuums floors, and washes down showers, because she is intentionally using her work as a way to worship and listen for God's promptings. Working alone in the presence of God casts the classic practice of solitude in a new light, illuminating the work produced in solitude in a new way.

Working in solitude was important in the life of David, who eventually became the king of Israel. In his early years, David tended his family's sheep in the fields by himself. During this season of working alone, he learned how to protect his own flock and began to understand the Lord as the Good Shepherd. In this time of solitary work, David wrote worship music and developed the trusting relationship with God that created the courage and character he needed later in life to do more significant things. Slaying a giant, serving as a royal advisor, fleeing from those who wanted him dead, leading a country in war and in peace, and directing his people toward proper worship of God—all have their humble beginnings in his early times of solitary work.

Jesus' many miracles are another example of working in the presence of God. Jesus was not always—or even typically—alone when he healed, transformed, or forgave. And yet, there was a sense in each of the signs he performed of a deep connection to God the Father, whose power worked through him to effect supernatural changes. As Jesus worked, the presence of God brought about the results in his ministry.

## Involuntary Solitude

Lastly, we must acknowledge that sometimes solitude is not by choice. Some people are forced into times of isolation, which may not be what they would desire or choose for themselves. This can happen when you're reassigned to a new department where you don't know anyone or you're given a task that allows you little interaction with others. Perhaps you are stuck in your office for days on end, while your coworkers go out to meet with clients. Or you may have been injured on the job and find yourself alone while you recover. You may be laid off—without choice—and you find yourself at home, without coworker interactions. These circumstances can be involuntary experiences with solitude—which can feel more like solitary confinement or even exile.

We see scriptural examples of this type of solitude: Joseph was put into prison and forgotten for a long time. Elijah spent years by himself during a drought, with no one for company except the ravens who brought him food. Jonah was swallowed by a fish and found himself truly alone in the depths. None of them experienced their solitude as pleasant, but God had a distinct purpose for each one. During this time alone, in the recesses of the quiet, each person hears from God in ways they would not have without the involuntary experience of solitude.

If you are experiencing solitude and do not want to be, take heart from the stories of those in Scripture who have suffered through this. It means God is at work! God is trying to get your attention, and God wants to use this time to prepare you for what is in store for you. God wants to use this time to speak to you. Seek to embrace this season with an openness for God to provide what you need, rather than what you think you need. Since you don't know how God might change you, look for how God might surprise you!

The complete aloneness Jesus experienced on the cross is the most significant example in Scripture, and unlike any we will ever know. While we will never be abandoned by God the Father, Jesus' experience of being forsaken brought about our reconciliation with God. This being forsaken by the Father—which Jesus was willing to experience fully, even to the depths of hell itself—ensured that we will never experience this type of alienation ourselves.

When we come into seasons of isolation, and most of us will at one point or another, we know we have a Savior who has experienced the loneliness, despair, and heartbreak of this experience. As the author of Hebrews says, "For we do not have a high priest who is unable to empathize with our weaknesses, but we have one who has been tempted in every way, just as we are—yet he did not sin" (Heb. 4:15). Jesus' suffering complete aloneness provides for us the companionship of a friend, advocate, and guide in our own times of involuntary solitude. For many, this is when Jesus' companionship becomes a deeper friendship than they may ever have experienced before.

## STORIES OF SOLITUDE

### Jeff's Story

After fifteen years of working in a large corporate law firm, Jeff was awarded a three-month sabbatical (or as the firm more accurately characterized it, an "extended vacation"). During the course of this sabbatical, Jeff planned a lengthy trip with his family to England and a two-week vacation with his wife in the South Pacific. But then he recognized that it would be better if he began the sabbatical with a week alone. So on the first day, Jeff drove five hours and checked into a monastery in the next state.

It was quiet—indeed, disquietingly so. After the frantic push to make sure his caseload was ready for his three-month absence, the sudden stop coupled with virtually no opportunities for conversation was disorienting. At first, Jeff wondered if he would last the week. He had only brought a couple of books and an empty journal. How would he possibly fill the time?

But then Jeff discovered a new rhythm. When the monks gathered in the sanctuary six times a day to chant the Psalms, Jeff joined them. He took long, slow, quiet walks around the grounds. Mimicking the monks, Jeff stopped running or even walking fast. He "strolled." Jeff discovered what it was like to have a rhythm of work and prayer wrapped in extended periods of solitude. He could feel the rush of adrenaline subsiding. His journaling was slower but deeper, sometimes accompanied by spasms of joy and sometimes by tears. By the time he returned home, he found himself centered as if he had taken an extended shower to wash away years of frantic noise. From this posture of silence, he was more present to his family and more present to God.

## Uli's Story

Uli was the CEO of a computer software company, and his life was full with the demands and challenges of the business. One year as part of a Lenten discipline, he decided to spend early mornings in solitude in his home office, away from the demands of work for a period of time. He began each morning simply by paying attention to the world around him. As part of this practice, he chronicled his thoughts in "stream of consciousness" writing in a journal. He found himself quite surprised by the material that flowed out; the freedom he experienced in not using the kind of structured and organized thought his work required, as well as the regularity of the practice each day, were both useful in shaping his experience of solitude.

In reflecting on this practice a few years later, Uli referred to it as "a time of 'drinking at the Well of Life' and regaining a larger perspective for my life and work." It not only provided a renewed perspective but also an integrated wholeness to that season of his life, which had often been disorienting and fragmented.

The following reflection emerged from Uli's practice one day. It provides some insight into the power of solitude for shaping Uli's experience of God before his workday began.[2]

*The darkness before the coming day. A room filled with light in anticipation of a light-filled day that requires no effort to illuminate.*

*An enclave of light. A protected place where we can truly be ourselves—although that too is harder than it should be. Why is being who we are so difficult? The temptation to be something and someone other than ourselves, shaped in the image of the One Who made us, is systemic in the world. "Don't let the world squeeze you into its own mold."*

*How do we live faithfully, simply ourselves? What nourishes our core identity as Image of God, beings not artificially distorted into a parody of ourselves?*

*The lighted room. The place to see ourselves as we were intended to be with no distortion. An accurate reflection of the Reflection.*

> *Give us grace to see,*
> *to not mock ourselves*
> *with falsehood.*
> *Teach us to care*
> *and not to care.*
> *Teach us to sit still*
> *even among these rocks*
> *Our peace in His will.*

## THE PRACTICE OF SOLITUDE

These three types of solitude can be practiced in various ways depending on your vocation, your schedule, and your season of life and faith. Here are a few examples of how to navigate these practices—but also a few warnings before you begin.

First, it can be tempting to have strong expectations for what you might experience during times of solitude. Resist this urge. God will meet you most significantly where your need is greatest, not necessarily in the way you desire. Allow there to be freedom for the Holy Spirit to work, without setting yourself up for disappointment with God. Second, what you experience during solitude is not better or worse than what you experience while engaging in the other spiritual practices. Third, be creative. Long periods of solitude are not feasible for all vocations and stages of life. Be imaginative about how you might practice this—while a baby or toddler is sleeping in the car, on a night when the family is otherwise occupied and you have a night alone, or when you are asked to do an errand for work that is not normally in your job description. These practices are meant to serve you and your working life; you are not meant to serve the practice.

## Time Alone Listening to God

Set aside a designated amount of time based on your needs and the needs of those in your life (family members, coworkers, and so on). This could be an hour, a half day, a day, or a few days. Structure this time alone for rest, reflection, listening, and discerning. Being intentional about this time will help guide your solitude. The Latin phrase *ora et labora* ("pray and work"), which became the motto for St. Benedict's Rule, may be helpful. Consider the ways in which your prayer and work intertwine. Your work can be a form of prayer. Conversely, let your solitude be a time where prayer itself—connecting in conversation with God—becomes your work.

As you move into solitude, give yourself space simply to rest. Solitude is not part of the natural rhythm of life for most of us, and so getting to solitude may require frantically working to finish everything in order to take time away. Allow your heart to slow to a quieter pace. Take a nap, take a walk, take in your surroundings, or just take some deep breaths.

Next, enter into a time of reflection on your work or whatever else God may be pulling your attention toward. The Prayer of Examen (in chapter 10) may be a good starting place. Review what has been happening in your life, your work, your relationships, and your own soul. The examen can provide structure for those whose minds wander or as a starting place for entering into that time of solitude.

After engaging in the Prayer of Examen, you may want to rest, be quiet, and just be. Including time to do nothing during solitude may feel frivolous, but it will open you to being able to listen to what the Lord has to say to you. Listen for the voice of the Good Shepherd. What is it that God wants to speak to you about? How might you enter into conversation as you listen? How might God desire you to respond?

Lastly, use some time to discern what your next step should be concerning your work. Take what God has revealed to you during this time and dialog with him about how you can engage your everyday work differently. What changes need to be made? What messages need to be conveyed? How might you reenter your life with a renewed sense of God's presence and guidance?

### Working Alone in God's Presence

The practice and application of this type of solitude will be different from the one just outlined. Working alone in the presence of God occurs in the context of your everyday working life. You may have an office space, a communal workspace, a classroom, or a vehicle where you do your work. Using this space, intentionally engage God in prayer. Begin your work by first becoming aware of God's presence with you. Centering prayer, where a few minutes at a time you repeat a phrase or a verse, can help you enter into this awareness. Simply repeating "I am loved unconditionally by God" or "God is with me as I work" or "Work and prayer, prayer and work" with each breath you take during these few minutes can be a way of acknowledging God's presence with you as you work.

Next, begin your work seeking to remain in a prayerful disposition as you do. Again, the phrase *ora et labora* can be helpful here. This time, however, you are seeking to understand how your work itself can be a prayer. How you go about actually doing your work can be prayerful. Performing your work well can be an offering of worship. Consult God as you work, listen for the response, and then act on what you have heard.

Every so often you may want to set a timer, a reminder on your phone, or some other way to pause while working, in order to remind yourself of the truth that God is with you in your work and desires to accomplish his purposes through you. Depending on how long you work alone, this could be done in fifteen-minute increments, hourly increments, or every several hours. Do what you need to remain in regular awareness of the Holy Spirit's presence with you, moving through you as you become a channel for God's presence in the world.

At the end of your work in solitude, again take a few minutes in prayer. This could be done on the way home from work, on a walk outside during a break, or another time that fits your schedule and your vocation. Use this time to thank God for the presence of the Holy Spirit, work to do, the Lord's counsel and aid in your work, and the ways in which this practice shaped who you are as a Christian worker.

### Involuntary Solitude

While involuntary solitude is not a choice, it can still be practiced with intention. When you enter into a season of isolation, there are few ways you can take this time and turn it into a practice of engaging with God.

First, if the solitude is not welcomed, enter into some lament with the Lord. Chapter 8 discusses this practice extensively, but be honest with God about your solitude. Having a conversation with God about your feelings and experiences is crucial to inviting him to use the time of isolation to form you.

Second, ask what desires the Lord has for you during this time. Again, laying out your lament will be helpful in clearing the way for being open to listening to what God may say to you. Some questions that may be helpful to guide this conversation include: What am I to learn during this season? What change needs to take place in me so God can use me differently? How might God desire to come near me during this season? Who needs me and my story right now?

Third, be intentional about not filling up the time of involuntary solitude with busyness. Sometimes when we are in a season in which we rather would not be, we hide behind filling our schedules instead of facing what God might be doing in and through our lives. Keep hours and even days open on purpose to intentionally converse with God in prayer about your unemployment, your injury, your isolation, or other reason you are experiencing involuntary solitude. Allowing time to be honest about where you are will provide a way forward into a new life—and a deeper connection with God.

Lastly, take advantage of this time to enter into some of the other practices in this book. When we are busy and our schedules are overly full, it is easy to find excuses not to connect with God. You now have the time to be intentional in engaging with God about your work. For even in a involuntary season of solitude, there is still work—although it will likely be different from what you are used to doing.

## QUESTIONS FOR REFLECTION OR DISCUSSION

1. *Are there regular times in your work in which you work alone? What does this time look like for you? How might you engage intentionally in working alone in the presence of God?*

2. *What has been your history with solitude? What place has it held for you in your working life? In your faith? How has God revealed his character to you through solitude?*

3. *When have you experienced a time of involuntary solitude? How did you navigate through that season? What did God reveal to you during that time?*

4. *What other practices in this book can be incorporated into your practice of solitude? When will you set aside intentional time to be in the presence of God for rest, reflection, and rejuvenation?*

# 10

# PRAYER OF EXAMEN FOR WORK

We spend much of our lives in the minutia of tasks and projects. The day-in/day-out world of never-ending lists and meetings can keep us looking so closely at what we need to do next that we miss what else might be going on: how we are being formed, and how God is at work.

We miss celebrating small successes, because the pressure of producing more weighs heavily on us. We miss opportunities to extend grace to those on our teams, because we are so focused on our individual responsibilities. We miss God's voice during our interactions with others or in the midst of projects, as we begin to hold too tightly to how our work should turn out. In missing these opportunities to hear God's voice, we begin to think and act as if the results of the work God has called us to are all up *to us*. When we begin carrying the burden of our work on our own shoulders, we come to believe that we are not co-laborers at all—but rather sole laborers, isolated and alone, set on serving the work no matter the cost.

As Christians, we believe that God is at work in our days, hours, and even our moments. We do not, however, always see God's activity. Like a child playing hide-and-seek on a sunny day, we may see the shadows of God's movements but wonder about the path God took or where he is going. We are called to live wide-awake to the activity of God, having the spiritual eyesight and insight to see where God is at work. This is not an easy endeavor, though. We must learn to train our hearts and minds to be attentive to seeing our Lord in this intimate, moment-to-moment way.

We are called not to go through life sleepwalking—just going through the motions—but as people awake to the actions of God in our midst. The examen is an ancient practice that can aid us in this wide-awake life. By practicing daily reflection on where we saw God at work or even where we missed God's activity, we awaken to the reality of God's presence around us and through us. This is the heart of the practice of the examen, paying attention and being alert to the activity of God in our everyday lives. As we become attuned to the presence of God, we also become more aware of God's longing to be in relationship with us.

## LIVING WIDE-AWAKE

The Examen for Work systematically explores what happened in our workday. In the examen we look at, turn over, and see from all directions the events that we experienced throughout the day. Reviewing these events allows us to notice and pay attention to the conversations we had, what we are grateful for, the interactions or tasks that irritated us, and our emotions at work. We also identify when we heard from God and, just as importantly, when we missed God, failed to recognize the Lord's activity, or intentionally pushed God away. The examen is an examination of our life "with God."[1] It is an echo of the longing of David the psalmist, who said,

> Search me, God, and know my heart;
>     test me and know my anxious thoughts.
> See if there is any offensive way in me,
>     and lead me in the way everlasting. (Ps. 139:23–24)

Richard Foster writes, "The examen . . . is the means God uses to make us more aware of our surroundings."[2] Engaging in the Prayer of Examen for work on a regular basis trains our minds and hearts to pay attention to God in different ways. We come to know the character of the Lord, and we experience firsthand the ways in which God is at work in us and through us—connecting us to God's activity in the world in deeper ways.

In the examen, we create the habit of being thankful, curious about where God is at work, and open to listening to where we may have missed God's presence. Taking time to reflect on the day as it has just passed, we learn to savor the moments, events, and interactions in our ordinary lives. This savoring leads us to joy in the Lord. As the Jesuit priest James Martin said,

> Savoring is the antidote to our increasingly rushed lives. . . . Savoring slows us down. In the examen we do not recall an important experience simply to add it to a list of things we have seen or done; rather we savor it as if it were a satisfying meal. We pause to enjoy what has happened. It's a deepening of our gratitude to God, revealing the hidden joys of our days.[3]

For Saint Ignatius, who popularized the practice in the sixteenth century,[4] the examen becomes a way of living life *before* God, *with* God, and *in* God's Spirit. In fact, he encouraged his fellow Jesuit brothers that, if they omitted any type of prayer during their day, they should not skip the Prayer of Examen. It was that important! For Ignatius, the examen became a way of being with God in the midst of his life, not simply another prayer or one more task to check off his list during the day. The presence of God that he experienced during his time of praying the examen became so precious to him that omitting it was not an option in his life.

## THE HEART OF THE EXAMEN

The Latin meaning for the word *examen* conveys the idea of "an accurate assessment of the true situation."[5] Praying the examen reminds us that God desires to be in relationship with us and that we are designed to be in relationship with God. Consistently setting aside time each day to practice this examination will build your ability to pay attention and discover what you missed from God during the day. You may see where your relationship with God was broken during the day. You may see the ways you need to say you are sorry. As David says in Psalm 139:1,

> You have searched me, LORD,
>   and you know me.

This practice opens our spiritual eyes, not only to connect with God as he reveals more about the reality of our lives, but also to see God's amazing grace and his longing to be in relationship with us. Through the examen, we trust that God knows us better than we know ourselves, and that he is able to reveal to us what we cannot know on our own.

As you practice the examen, you will find that not only do you see God's activities in the rearview mirror of your life, but that you also begin to look for and see them in surprising places in the present. Paradoxically, by retrospectively looking for God's fingerprints over our days, we begin to experience the presence of God in each moment. As we pursue God, we find that God has been pursuing us, and this pursuit is cause for celebration and joy. Can you imagine what your working life would look like if it were filled with the joy of the Lord on a daily basis? This is what can happen when you deliberately examine your life before God!

As you begin the habit of making careful examination of your life, you will start to see how God works in and wants to be a part of your everyday life. This may be different from how God works in others' lives. By paying attention to God's work in *your* life, however, you will start to notice patterns you may not have seen before. For instance, you might recognize that a growing irritation at work is a way the Lord is trying to develop a certain virtue in your character. Or you might notice that you enjoy projects, conversations, and tasks associated with a certain topic or that are repetitive and result in a tangible outcome—or perhaps the opposite! Exploring these observations with God through the examen will deepen your understanding of yourself, as well as deepening your experience of and relationship with God at work.

Pay attention to whatever comes up repeatedly during your time of examen. If your interactions with a particular coworker regularly come to mind as you reflect with God about your day, then you may want to have a conversation with God about how you could be generous, loving, and kind toward this person. Things that you hear repeatedly may be God's way of guiding, directing, and leading you. Making the examen a part of your daily life with God will lead you not only into deeper relationship with Christ, but it will also reveal God's characteristic movements in your days. The fingerprints of God's activity are revealed as we notice how, when, and where God is at work in and through our working lives.

## A WORD OF CAUTION

Here, however, is a warning. For people who are used to working in the world of tasks and to-do lists, the examen can turn into something else to check off your list. You may start to practice the examen in a way that mimics your own need for productivity, going through the examen like just another list to get through. Do not give in to this temptation. Remember that the examen is prayed in the presence of God and is an act of being with God. During the examen, we rely on God to bring things to mind and show us the truth of our experiences, where God is at work, and the state of our soul. When we undertake the examen with only the power of our own observations and scrutiny, we can find ourselves subjected to self-criticism and overwhelmed with despair. This is not what God wants for us. God wants to be with us. Instead, as Richard Foster describes comfortingly, when we see our sins "under the searching light of the great Physician . . . [we] can expect only good always."[6]

## THE EXAMEN FOR WORK

What might happen when we step back to look at and intentionally reflect upon what we might have missed, while staring so intently at the tasks before us? How might you practice the examen in your working life? A typical examen has several sections. In this chapter, we will focus on a five-section Prayer of Examen for work—focusing on gratitude, review, sorrow, forgiveness, and grace. By reflecting with God on each of these areas on a regular basis, you will begin to see God's provision and blessing surrounding your work, as well as your own sin and lack of obedience toward God in your work. Think of the examen for work like looking through a magnifying glass: it will magnify both the blessings and the challenges in the context of God's loving care. When we see things clearly in the light of this gracious love, we are drawn into God's parental embrace, helped and surrounded by the wisdom and care of the Lord.

Our explanation of the practical side of the examen is a starting point. You may find that a question or a section becomes particularly important, and you may decide to spend additional time on that point. What is needed in the examen is a heart ready to pay attention and see what God might bring up. If some section of the examen is particularly meaningful during a certain season, then allow yourself to spend extra time there. The practice is not meant to be followed slavishly, but rather it is a gift that allows us to see where God is seeking us out at work. Allow the examen to be used for that purpose: not as another task to get through, but as a way of living your life wide-awake to the activity of God's Spirit in your work and your life.

# FIVE SECTIONS OF THE EXAMEN

## *Gratitude*

We begin the examen with gratitude. Becoming grateful for the blessings of your work, from the minute to the obvious, begins to open up a wellspring of vision in your life. Where you may have been stuck in frustration and disappointment, beginning with an attitude of thankfulness can bring about a whole new way of viewing your work. Gratitude enables us to see where God is moving, even in the midst of situations that might seem hopeless. Gratitude can be the friction that creates the traction for change in our lives, and it can transform how we approach our work in the following days.

In beginning with gratitude, we find ourselves thankful to God for the ways he is indeed at work and how he might be blessing our lives. In gratitude, we offer God's good gifts to us back as an offering; and in doing so, we emulate David in Psalm 9:1–2, proclaiming,

> *I will give thanks to you, Lord, with all my heart;*
>> *I will tell of all your wonderful deeds.*
> *I will be glad and rejoice in you;*
>> *I will sing the praises of your name, O Most High.*

## *Review*

We often miss what happens in our days. We start the day with a list of tasks a mile long, and we end the day exhausted from meetings, interactions, travel, caretaking, and other things the day required of us. We might want to forget the day at its close. Maybe it is a day you do not wish to relive. And yet, reviewing the day can reveal where God was at work in deeper ways and was calling you toward himself. The review section is a way of raising an Ebenezer, which means "Thus far the Lord has helped us," as Samuel did with a stone after defeating the Philistines (1 Sam. 7:12). When we review our day before God we recognize and acknowledge, "Lord, here is where you met me and helped me."

Allow this time to be fun! It may seem a little dull at the beginning: "First, I got in my car, then I drove to work, then I did such and such a task," and so on. No matter how seemingly mundane, chronologically go through your day and then start asking God where he was at work and where you may have missed him. This is where the fun begins: Like a child finding a toy she didn't know she was missing, this practice will result in some "aha!" moments. You may find yourself excited to see what God brings up during your review. Be on the lookout for God to show you "the wonders of your great love" (Ps. 17:7). By reviewing the day that has passed, you will begin to see the ways in which God's great love met you along the way.

On the other hand, you may not think it's fun to find God meddling in the affairs of *your* day. Pay attention to this as well. What does that reveal to you about what might need to change in your relationship with God? Regardless, reviewing your day is a critical part of becoming more aware of God's presence in your working life.

## Sorrow

In this section, you will take whatever God brought to your attention during the review that were areas of sin and bring them into God's presence. Was there an instance during the day where you deliberately ignored the Holy Spirit's leading? Confess that to God. Or did your own conscience seek to warn you about something that you ignored? Talk to God about it. Maybe you participated in something you knew was not ethical. Maybe you blamed someone else for a mistake you made. Perhaps you showed favoritism to an employee or did not act respectfully to a client or a colleague. Maybe you worked with an attitude from which God has called or with an attitude you know is not what the Lord desires for you. Or perhaps you ignored God today in order to gain popularity, esteem, or standing at work.

It may not seem that spending time thinking about your misdeeds will feel good—we do not typically think of sorrow as a positive experience! However, there is a "grace of sorrow"[7] that God gives as we begin to bring these moments in our day into God's presence. With God's help, we begin to be truly sorry for whatever is counter to God's purposes, we begin to see the world as God sees it, and we begin to desire what God desires. We can use David's words from Psalm 32:5 and confess to God,

> *Then I acknowledged my sin to you*
> *and did not cover up my iniquity.*
> *I said, "I will confess*
> *my transgressions to the Lord."*
> *And you forgave*
> *the guilt of my sin.*

It is only through this sorrow for what is counter to God's intentions that we begin to experience God's best. And so the sorrow itself is grace from God.

## Forgiveness

The purpose of seeking the "grace of sorrow" is not to wallow in our shortcomings and sins, but rather to seek the forgiveness of our loving Savior and turn toward and heal the broken relationship. Without Christ we can do nothing, so even forgiveness is a gift we need to receive from God. During this time, we bring the sins from the sorrow section and ask God for the grace of forgiveness and a clean slate to begin again the next day.

Think of the portraits of Jesus in the Gospels in which he tells ordinary people to go, "your sins are forgiven" (Matt. 5; Mark 7; Luke 2). Jesus calls the people he heals—physically and spiritually—to go. There is a call to action in God's forgiveness. It is a call not to wallow in the sin, but to accept God's gift of forgiveness and go live as a forgiven person. While we may struggle with similar things today as we did yesterday, the experience of God's forgiveness propels us back into our lives, enabling us to live in freedom and hope. We work as forgiven and blessed people. As David proclaims in Psalm 32:1–2,

> Blessed is the one
>> whose transgressions are forgiven,
>> whose sins are covered.
> Blessed is the one
>> whose sin the LORD does not count against them
>> and in whose spirit is no deceit.

## Grace

After receiving forgiveness for the ways in which we fell short, we now can turn toward the last section of the examen. In this section, we begin looking toward the next day. After we are grateful for the gifts of this day, review the day, and identified areas in which we fell short and then asked forgiveness, we now seek God's grace to live differently tomorrow. The examen highlights God's desire to engage with us, as well as Christ's power to transform us for our work the next day. How we are able to change is, of course, all God's doing—for indeed we can do nothing without his help and grace (John 15:5). In this section of the examen, we express this truth back to God: We need God's Spirit to change us.

This need may be especially salient during seasons of conflict or organizational change or when learning a new job or joining a new team. During new or difficult seasons, it is easy to recognize that we do not have all we need for our work, and so we must approach our tasks with the humility and grace we can receive only from our Savior. On the other hand, it may be even more important that we seek grace to change when we find ourselves working in confidence and with experience. It is then, especially, that we need to rely on the strength of God, lest we become caught in the trap of pride and think our work is simply that: all ours.

The truth is that we are co-laborers in Christ's work in the world, no matter what our vocation and no matter how long we have been at it. The grace to change and the grace to see the day ahead as covered by God is something each of us needs to experience daily. Just as we need to seek the grace of sorrow, we also need God's grace to show us the ways in which we can think, feel, act, and be different for the day ahead. Using the questions of the examen, we can call on God and request divine help, and hear his loving words in reply (Ps. 32:8),

> *I will instruct you and teach you in the way you should go;*
> *I will counsel you with my loving eye on you.*

## HOW WILL I FIND THE TIME?

If your life is particularly full—with obligations to work, family, church, and community—it may feel overwhelming to think about how you will find time to participate in the practice of examen. We understand this sentiment. Carving away time for these practices takes discipline, knowledge of our own lives and schedules, and a willingness to create boundaries for the sake of being formed. Actually, participating in the examen may be a way of marking your days in a way that forms you differently. Over time you may see, as Saint Ignatius did, that you actually cannot afford *not* to engage in this practice—for the ways it is transforming you and your relationship with God. With that said, here are a few suggestions for how you might find time to engage in this practice:

- *Use the final ten minutes of the workday to explore the examen in your workspace.*

- *Engage in an examen while commuting home from work. Consider using it in conjunction with the "Liturgy of Commute" in chapter 1.*

- *If you have a regular exercise schedule after work, use some of this time to reflect on the questions of the examen.*

- *Use the first ten to fifteen minutes after getting home from work to go through the examen (this may be harder for workers with young kids, but it may be a good transition away from work in the evening for others).*

- *Take ten to fifteen minutes before going to bed—the time you would usually be on your phone, watching television, or using some type of media—using that time instead to engage in the examen.*

- *Use ten minutes as you are getting ready for bed and brushing your teeth to go over the questions of the examen.*

## STORIES FROM THE PRAYER OF EXAMEN

### Cindy's Story

Cindy is a university librarian who began using the Prayer of Examen to observe where God was in her work. During her practice, she was reminded that God cares for her coworkers and the library patrons. This prompted her to be more intentional about engaging in positive and encouraging ways with each person. She began to practice holy listening when meeting with students, faculty, and staff, and by asking God to inhabit her classroom and lectures. The practice also nudged her to take time to pray over students while grading their papers.

Taking stock of her workday also prompted her to remember that God is present even in the drudgery of the day. Purchasing items and weeding out items from the library collection are responsibilities of her job that Cindy does not enjoy. But attending to a daily examen for a few weeks motivated her to begin praying over the work of deciding what items should be purchased and what items should be removed—a task particularly hard for Cindy. She decided that praying over what to buy and what to remove should become a regular practice. While she still experiences these tasks as onerous, knowing that God is present as she does the work gives it more meaning.

Over time, practicing the Prayer of Examen reminded Cindy that the work she does is holy work. The daily practice of reviewing her day provided a rhythm that caused her to take note of where God was present and where she had missed God. Cindy found that she was walking through her day with more peace, gratitude, and a strong awareness of God's presence. Reflecting on the day reminded her that God is desirous of a deeper relationship with her all day long, not just in church or at home.

### Greg's Story

Greg is a maintenance manager for a large property management company, whose job consists of traveling to different properties to assess and fix damages. Praying the examen has been especially impactful for Greg's work. It has helped him pay attention to the smaller details of his day and notice the ways the Holy Spirit is forming him as a Christian and as a worker.

As Greg used the examen for work, he began noticing his relationships with coworkers and tenants differently than he had before. Through paying attention and reviewing his day, Greg was able to put more effort into listening to the needs of those he serves—and spend less time talking at them. Listening well allowed him to respond more effectively, either with more useful actions or with words that better fit what God would want him to say.

Through the Prayer of Examen, Greg was stretched to pay attention to the ways in which his emotions affected his work. He would reflect on the feelings that arose throughout the day in his work and acknowledge these feelings by placing them before

God, trying to discern how God would have him respond. One day while looking for a roof leak, he stopped and lay down on his back, watching as the clouds passed overhead. Looking into the sky has a humbling power that makes our lives and problems seem small, compared to God's vastness. In those moments of lying on the roof, Greg experienced a strong sense of God's love, and he knew that he was cherished by God.

### Emily's Story

Emily is an assistant principal at an elementary school. The Prayer of Examen has been especially impactful for her as she works with students, teachers, and parents. So much of her working life includes moving from small problem to small problem and checking things off her list, trying to manage everything that makes the school operate. Her job is large with many complicated components, so when she came across the practice of examen, she wondered how it might impact her work.

One day, after engaging in the Prayer of Examen for a few weeks, she was helping a student who suffered from mental illness. Emily was injured while trying to prevent the student from self-harm. After her injury, she stopped praying through the examen for several weeks. It wasn't for lack of desire, but each time she came to the sorrow section of the examen, she felt blocked. She realized she had a choice. She could stay in the sorrow of the situation, or she could turn that sorrow over to God.

This was a turning point for Emily in her relationship with Christ and how she lives out that relationship in her work as at her school. Through the examen practice of acknowledging sorrow, she began to see that her own pride had led her to believe that it was up to her to save those around her who needed saving, instead of entrusting them to God. Ultimately, it was the practice of the examen that helped her move beyond sorrow into forgiveness and grace.

The last step of the examen—grace—helped Emily move on. Then, she found herself actually looking forward to experiencing God's presence in her work the next day. As she drove to the school, she was reminded of the promise of meeting God's new mercies each morning. Emily says, "When I tried to forgive myself, it was a dead end. But when I moved to hearing God's voice whisper his grace to me, it made the Prayer of Examen feel complete and sustaining, and I was able to accept God's forgiveness of me."

### Deb's Story

Deb works as a warehouse supervisor for an electric company, which involves many people doing many different jobs. When she first began at the company, her excitement for getting to know people was contagious. But over the years of working at the same location, in the same role, she began to feel that she was no longer heard by her boss or her coworkers. This created difficult interactions, and bitterness began to take root.

Practicing the Prayer of Examen, though, began to change that. As she allowed God to help her reflect on her day, she began to see those who worked in the warehouse differently. Because she was looking for ways that God might be at work, things that might once have annoyed her stopped bothering her as much. She began once again to take the time to stop at people's desks and take a genuine interest in how they were doing, knowing that God had placed them in her workplace for a reason.

Being attentive to the Holy Spirit throughout her workday also opened up conversations with her boss about ways the company could be involved and give back to the community, and she found her boss to be quite receptive to her ideas. Allowing God to speak into what happened in her work changed Deb's thoughts, intentions, and behaviors, reminding her that it was ultimately the Lord for whom she was working.

## THE PRACTICE OF EXAMEN FOR WORK

As you practice the examen, you should spend time in each of the five sections we discussed in this chapter: Gratitude, Review, Sorrow, Forgiveness, and Grace. It is not, however, necessary to ask every question in each section. We provided a number of variations of these questions, and you may want to select only one or two specific ones that feel most relevant to you and your circumstances. Alternatively, you may want to come up with your own questions for each category.

You may want to write down your answers to the questions, but you certainly do not have to do so. Praying the examen can be done with a journal, but you can also engage in this prayer while doing something else physically. Some people pray the examen while shooting hoops in the driveway,[8] or while doing dishes. If you take a daily walk during a lunch break or in the afternoon, try using examen questions during this time. Remember that the heart of the examen is reviewing your days prayerfully in the presence of God. Find a way you can do this in the midst of your working life.

### Gratitude

Thinking about what you are grateful for should be less like making a list and more like "savoring a satisfying meal."[9] The goodness of God often becomes more apparent when we slow down and consciously reflect on all that he has given us. So let yourself savor, smile, and even laugh out loud at the ways God was present in this day. Savoring cannot be done quickly, so allow this entry into the examen to slow you. Let it be a calming time to remember God's presence with you. The following questions might be a good starting point toward entering into gratitude:[10]

1. *What are you grateful for today in your work?*

2. *Did an interaction, a project, task, conversation, or presentation go well? If so, then thank God for that.*

3. *Did you see God present in your work? What did that look like?*

4. *Who are you grateful for today and why?*

## Review

As you begin reviewing your day, pay attention to your emotions. Does a certain part of your day evoke emotion in you? If so, take note of that. God gave us emotions for a reason; they are our body's way of telling us something. Pay attention to the emotion and bring it to God. Simply asking "Lord, what does it mean that I feel this way about this interaction, meeting, or task?" may reveal to you something about yourself or about how God might be at work. Some of the following questions might be a starting point toward reviewing your day:

1. *What happened today? Begin reflecting chronologically through your day.*

2. *When did you struggle to say focused and engaged?*

3. *Where did you experience God's presence today?*

4. *Where did you miss God's presence today?*

5. *What were your interactions with your coworkers like? If you led others, how do you think these people experienced working with you?*

6. *When were you working at your best during the day? What made it your best work?*

7. *What did God reveal to you in this section that you need or desire to change for tomorrow?*

## Sorrow

We are often aware of what we are sorry for during the day. It could be something you did consciously or unintentionally, or something you left undone that you should have finished. Whatever you know was not God's best for you, acknowledge it during this time. Then ask for the "grace of sorrow" around these sins. God is the one who brings us to repentance, change, and transformation; you cannot change through your own efforts. God's grace is needed not only to know our sins but also to become sorry *and* sorrowful for the ways we have turned away from God. Ask for the grace to reorient your feelings around sinful actions or attitudes so they align with God's feelings.

If you are not feeling sorrowful, you may want to explore that with God. Let this section guide your reflection around why that may be, focusing on God's desires for you. Here are a few questions to help guide you through this time:

1. *Were there any ways in which you acted contrary to what you knew was right?*

2. *Were there situations where you heard God's prompting but chose to ignore it? If so, why?*

3. *Where are you experiencing sadness or sorrow over the ways in which you failed to love God today? What do those emotions tell you about God? What do those emotions tell you about yourself?*

4. *Where are you experiencing sadness or sorrow over the ways in which you failed to love others today? What is God calling you to do in response?*

## Forgiveness

Forgiveness draws the freshness of Christ into our lives, which can otherwise so easily become stuck in the mire of frustration, disappointment, and despair in our work. Entering and experiencing God's forgiveness on a daily basis prevents the sins of yesterday from meddling in the affairs of today. Here are some questions and steps to help you experience the forgiveness of God during this time:

1. *How might Christ want to forgive you for the ways you sinned? Where did you intentionally miss or refuse to follow God's leading?*

2. *Where is it difficult for you to accept Christ's forgiveness?*

3. *For what do you desire to be forgiven from the previous day?*

4. *Spend some time asking Jesus for forgiveness where you failed to listen to his voice in your work.*

5. *How do you experience God's forgiveness in this? Do certain words, phrases, or pictures come to mind?*

## Grace

This section of the examen will aid you in knowing God's grace and experiencing it in your life in tangible ways. In this section, you will ask God for the knowledge of the grace extended toward you and how you might live differently in light of what God revealed to you in the sorrow and forgiveness sections. You can then ask for the grace and virtue to live out that change. God may reveal to you a certain action to take, or he may also just tweak how you are feeling about the circumstances around the situation. Be open to how the change may occur and seek God's help to change. Here are some questions that may guide this time:

1. *After having reviewed the day, what do you feel God is calling you to change for tomorrow?*

2. *What changes do you desire to make in your communication, attitudes, demeanors, or work?*

3. *Are there changes you do not desire to make in your communication, attitudes, demeanors, or work? If so, why not?*

4. *What do you need from God in order to live out these changes? Pray for this.*

## QUESTIONS FOR REFLECTION OR DISCUSSION

Here are some questions to consider after you have prayed the examen for work for a week or two:

1. *Are there any aspects of your life that make it difficult for you to engage in examen? If so, what is your biggest challenge? What do you hear God saying to you about this?*

2. *What was the most surprising thing God brought to your attention while practicing examen?*

3. *In what areas of your work life does God seem to be showing up most consistently?*

4. *Which section of the examen created the most conversation with God? Which section was most difficult for you to go through? Why?*

5. *Were there any specific questions that were especially important for you personally?*

6. *Is your experience of God different when praying the examen than it is during other times of prayer? If so, in what ways?*

# 11

# SABBATH: CEASING FROM WORK

Everyone in the world is equal when it comes to time. Each of us is given the same allotment of twenty-four hours in a day and seven days in a week. But how we use our time varies dramatically. In North America, we tend to think about the work we need to accomplish in the time we have. Our culture venerates work. We value to do-lists, activities, and accomplishments. We thrive on productivity and often equate identity with how much we accomplish. When people ask how we're doing, many of us reply, "I'm really busy!" This kind of response demonstrates that somehow we think our busyness is equal with our worth. If we're busy, then our lives must mean something. And yet when we answer "I'm so busy," our souls reverberate something entirely different: exhaustion, burnout, lack of direction.

If you can relate to this sense of busyness, then you are not alone! According to a recent Gallup poll, the average workweek for Americans who work full time is forty-seven hours per week, and a quarter of salaried employees work sixty hours or more. These numbers have been rising steadily over the past two decades.[1] Outsiders to our culture often see this more clearly than we do. On a recent cab ride I (Denise) took, the driver—who had moved to the United States after growing up in Africa and living in Europe—commented, "When people here have a day off, they work."

Busyness has become our culture's addiction. As a society, we no longer know how to stop, how to enjoy the moment, and how to—well—rest. Or even how to rest well. The amount of time you spend working affects everything else in your life—your sleep, your vacation, your relationships, and your stress levels. In the mid-1800s, the average American got nine and a half hours of sleep each night.[2] By the mid-1900s, this dropped to eight hours, and today most of us average around seven hours.[3] If you are similar to many American workers, you regularly feel stressed out and you take stress home with you. You are likely to use only half of your vacation days; and when you do have a day off or go on vacation, you still work![4]

Technology has changed the landscape of our working lives entirely. While it promises to make life easier, when it comes to overwork, technology has actually made it worse. Instead of freeing you up to do more of what you like best, it may instead shackle you to your work or distract you from those who are right in front of you.

The way our culture thrives on ever-increasing productivity and frantic busyness does not fit well with God's intentions! From the beginning, God has modeled a different way. In the familiar creation account, God brought into being everything that exists in six days, and then he rested on the seventh (see Gen. 2:1–3). In some ways, this is a curious notion. Why does *God* rest? If we impose our own human experiences and limitations on God, then we might think that God is tired or needs to recharge his batteries. But this doesn't fit with the rest of Scripture or our understanding of an all-powerful God who does not "slumber or sleep" (Ps. 121:3–4). Instead, God's rest on the seventh day means something different. It communicates God's sovereignty over both creation and time itself.

There is a sense of tranquility and peace that comes from imagining God resting. He completed the creation. Everything necessary was provided for human flourishing, and God extended creative powers and authority to Adam and Eve in the Garden of Eden. His declaration of "It is very good!" brings with it connotations of complete overflowing goodness, as if he couldn't have put anymore more into his creation. And so, this resting is a profound statement that his creation was so good, it deserved to be savored.

This seventh-day rest also communicates God's dominion over time itself. God has created time, and he is above and beyond it in some unfathomable way. God did not need to rest, because he needed to catch up on sleep or because he had been working too hard the other six days. Rather, God's rest is a way for him to demonstrate power and, at the same time, model a life-giving habit for us.

This idea of resting on the seventh day is not just a nice idea that God models in the creation story. In case there is any doubt about whether or not humans are supposed to follow God's example of resting one day a week, God makes it clear: The notion of Sabbath rest is enshrined in the Ten Commandments, communicated by Moses to the Hebrew people escaping slavery in Egypt. While most Christians value the Ten Commandments as part of God's moral law, somehow the idea of Sabbath does not fit up there with not committing idolatry, stealing, or killing. Many of us have effectively taken the Ten Commandments and turned them into Nine Commandments plus One Suggestion.

Scripture seems to emphasize Sabbath rest in a way that most of us do not. In the Old Testament, the fourth commandment to keep the Sabbath is repeated regularly. We see it in Exodus when the story of Moses on Mount Sinai is first told (Exod. 20:8–11); we see it again in Deuteronomy when the Ten Commandments are reprised (Deut. 5:12–15); and we also see it referenced in Leviticus (Lev. 23:3).

## REST, REFLECTION, AND RELATIONSHIP

Scriptures that reference the Sabbath are quite distinct from one another. In particular, the rationale for keeping the Sabbath is different in each one. In the Exodus version, the Sabbath commandment is written as follows:

> Remember the Sabbath day by keeping it holy. Six days you shall labor
> and do all your work, but the seventh day is a Sabbath to the LORD
> your God. On it you shall not do any work, neither you, nor your son
> or daughter, nor your manservant or maidservant, nor your animals,
> nor the alien within your gates. For in six days the LORD made the
> heavens and the earth, the sea, and all that is in them, but he rested
> on the seventh day. Therefore the LORD blessed the Sabbath day and
> made it holy. (Exod. 20:8–11)

First, it is probably worth noting that the Sabbath day was not
just directed at the Hebrew people. They were to extend this day
to their servants, their animals, and to the foreigners living among
them. God's command to rest reaches through socioeconomic status,
societal rank, and even ethnic identity. The rationale that is given
for the Sabbath in this passage calls us back to creation. The Sabbath
is commanded, because God rested on the seventh day and made
it holy. The emphasis on this passage is on *rest*: The commandment is to rest because God rested. Because God savored, enjoyed
creation, and ceased from the act of creating more, we should also
savor, enjoy, and rest for our own making something of the world.

The parallel passage in Deuteronomy is somewhat altered.
While the command is basically the same, the reasoning here is
different:

> Observe the Sabbath day by keeping it holy, as the LORD your God
> has commanded you. . . . Remember that you were slaves in Egypt
> and that the LORD your God brought you out of there with a mighty
> hand and an outstretched arm. Therefore the LORD your God has com-
> manded you to observe the Sabbath day. (Deut. 5:12–15)

Instead of reminding the Hebrews of God's rest after creation, this
passage recalls their slavery in Egypt. The Hebrew people were told
to keep the Sabbath because God freed them from slavery. Part of
the commandment required them to *reflect* on God's power and
redeeming work. In Egypt, they had been forced to work every day

for long hours, without a promise of rest. With their freedom, God reminds them that they do not *have* to work all seven days; the Sabbath then becomes a gift to them. It is an opportunity to remember, a chance to reflect on the goodness of God in their midst, and a privilege to put away their productive pursuits. Imagine if we thought about Sabbath in the same way. Imagine a day where you stop working and use the time to reflect on God's power in your own life. What would a day to stop and savor look like for you?

The third passage that references the Sabbath commandment is found in Leviticus.

> There are six days when you may work, but the seventh day is a Sabbath of rest, a day of sacred assembly. (Lev. 23:3)

This time, the description of the fourth commandment has a different connotation. The rationale given for keeping the Sabbath in this passage is so the people can gather together in sacred assembly. The Sabbath gives us space to gather with others in community and to worship God. Time to pursue *relationships* with others and with God is facilitated by keeping the Sabbath.

These three ideas of rest, reflection, and relationship, embedded in the Old Testament Scriptures about the Sabbath, can shape our understanding of how God intended us to experience Sabbath—as a gift from God designed to meet our physical, emotional, and spiritual needs.

## Sabbath Rest

So what exactly is the Sabbath anyway? The Hebrew word we translate means "to stop," "to cease," or "put to an end." Throughout history, the Jews have practiced the Sabbath from sundown on Friday to sundown on Saturday—twenty-four hours of no work. Many Christians have adopted Sunday as a Sabbath day, because it is a day that memorializes Jesus' resurrection.[5] Regardless, the scriptural idea of the Sabbath involves one twenty-four-hour period during which we set aside productive work and create space for rest, worship, and play.

Jesus was often challenged by the Pharisees about his own Sabbath practices. They criticized his disciples for picking grain to eat on the Sabbath, and then they criticized Jesus himself for healing people on the Sabbath (Matt. 12:1–14). While Jesus seems to reject the particularity of the Pharisees' rules about what activities are or are not allowed on the Sabbath, he does not reject the Sabbath itself. Rather, he reinforces that the Sabbath is made for humans, rather than humans for law-keeping and Sabbath-keeping (see Mark 2:27).

We often miss the point that Sabbath-keeping is a great gift! Jesus communicates that the Sabbath is not simply one more rule to remember and follow, but rather it is a blessing that God designed and gave to us. It is out of God's abundance that he rested. The Creator of the universe did not need to rest and recharge because he was tired. No, he rested out of a desire to experience the goodness of creation.

If we feel some obligation to rest out of sheer desire to keep the law, then we need to go back to the source of the Sabbath, the Gift-giver himself and remember that the Sabbath was not given to prevent us from doing our work, but as a gift for us as his children.

There are many reasons to think that practicing the Sabbath is indeed a gift from God. Resting on the Sabbath reinforces the idea that we have the opportunity (and freedom) one day a week to choose to stop working; we are not slaves to our work. Paradoxically, when we choose to walk away from demands of work for one day a week—when we give up our control over our circumstances and job demands to God—it is at this moment of releasing control that we find real agency. When we take time to rest, we realize we have control over our time, rather than always letting time control us. In observing the Sabbath, we do not run away from our work, but we cease letting it dictate our lives.[6]

The Sabbath can be the catalyst for moving our souls away from the frantic hurry of our culture and toward rest in God's lap. So what is the state of your soul? Is it grounded and steady, so that even when you are busy, your life is full but not fractured? Or is it hurried and you're fearful that you're never going to get everything done, that you're always distracted by those never-ending tasks, which means that you're never *present*? The habit of stopping work on a regular basis is the antidote for a hurried soul.

Taking time away from work also reminds us of where our true worth lies. We are not valuable because of what we do or because of what we manage to achieve. We are valuable because God loves us and created us in his divine image. When we cease work, we remind ourselves that the world can get along without us. This can be something of a surprise for those who have high levels of work responsibility. Sabbath rest nudges us toward the truth that God values us for who we are, rather than for what we do. We cannot earn God's favor, but we can rest in knowing that our identity is in Christ.

Sabbath rest involves stopping our work. So we know what we should *not* be doing. But what are we supposed *to do* on that day? Here, the Old Testament Scriptures that emphasize the Sabbath as an opportunity for reflection and relationship can guide us.

### Sabbath Reflection

The Hebrews were told that on the Sabbath they should "remember" that they had been slaves and that God had rescued them from Egypt. The Sabbath is an opportunity to notice the ways that God is at work in the world. Eugene Peterson writes that the "Sabbath is that uncluttered time and space in which we can distance ourselves from our own activities enough to see what God is doing."[7]

Another way that the Sabbath is a gift is that it reminds us that we are not in control. To some, that may not feel much like a gift.

But because God is in control, all the world, including our corners of the world, don't hang in the balance because of what we do, or fail to do, in our work.

Work often blows our sense of responsibility out of proportion. We come to see ourselves as integral to the outcomes of our organizations. The Sabbath reminds us that our work can go on without us. Yes, we are valuable to our work, but ultimately God is the one holding our work, our teams, and our organizations together. Not us! In Colossians 1:16–17, Paul shouts this truth to us:

> For in him all things were created: things in heaven and on earth, visible and invisible, whether thrones or powers or rulers or authorities; all things have been created through him and for him. He is before all things, *and in him all things hold together*. (Italics added)

Paul speaks of God as the originator of *all things*. As the creator, inventor, and source of all things, God also holds all things together. God holds the details of your relationships at work, the details of the big project on which you are working, and the details of how you will make ends meet this month.

The Sabbath propels us toward deeper faith—believing that God is taking care of us, that our work will be there after a day of rest, and that God will continue to hold everything in the balance while we choose rest over productivity. This gift not only propels us toward a life of faith, but it also gives us the opportunity to reflect on the state of our souls during the work week. Some questions for reflection during this time include: To what have you been a slave? From what has God rescued you? What is God doing in your life? Where have you seen God's power and goodness expressed in your circumstances?

The Sabbath provides time to reflect on God's goodness: to recognize your blessings, and to be content in your circumstances. As the psalmist writes,

*Give thanks to the LORD, for he is good.*
   *His love endures forever. . . .*
*To him who alone does great wonders,*
   *His love endures forever. (Ps. 136:1, 4)*

Practicing the Sabbath also provides an opportunity to evaluate your choices ahead. In this future-oriented time of reflection, you can ask: What is God calling you to do in the week ahead? How might it be infused with God's energy? How might your work be changed by God's presence? What might God want to do through you?

But you can't reflect in this way if you are busy, tired, overwhelmed, or distracted. Have you ever heard someone tell you that they were just too busy to think? Often this is after they have done something they wish they hadn't (or not done something they wish they had). The Sabbath can provide an antidote to this level of unthinking busyness. It allows you the opportunity to reflect and to live a thoughtful life with integrity.

### Sabbath Relationship—With Others

Setting aside work one day a week also opens up the possibility for relationships with others. It allows time for meals with friends, games with family members, naps with a spouse, or outdoor activities. While most of us recognize the benefits of relationships for relationship's sake, connecting with others has benefits beyond just friendships. Research shows that healthy interpersonal relationships can minimize the experience of stress, support physical healing, increase longevity, and create a positive sense of well-being.[8]

Relating with people without the demands of work weighing on us enables us to be present to those around us. As part of Sabbath practice, some have put their phones away so as to be relieved of distraction.

The Sabbath day can also be a time for engaging with each other through play. It can be a time for laughter, running, jumping, and playing outside. It can be a time for re*creation* (did you catch the concept of "creation" embedded in that word?). Hop on a bike, break out the tennis racquet, pull out a board game, or go for a walk. Playing allows us to enter into a different, slower pace—a pace that can involve playing for its own sake. This different pace slows us down so that we can enjoy God's creation, as well as God's own playfulness with us. In this way, we remind ourselves that we weren't meant to be worked into the ground, but that God himself is one who is continuously at play in the creation.[9]

What a gift God embeds for us in the Sabbath! Why not engage in it?

### Sabbath Relationship—With God

Perhaps most obviously, the Sabbath allows us a day to focus attention on our relationship with God. For many, we engaged in this during a corporate worship gathering. While some—pastors and church staff—may have work responsibilities at church, most of us enter into this time of worship, not only as a way to rest but also as a way to reflect and bring our experience of work into the worship gathering. This allows for a bigger sense of purpose and meaning in life, and also for a space where we can hear from the Holy Spirit about what might be happening at work. Worship should not be divorced from our work: in fact, we should offer up our work to God.

There are some who may not be able to participate in a corporate worship gathering on a regular basis. This includes those who are infirm, those whose work interferes with worship times, and those who have intense caregiving responsibilities. People in these situations (and their church communities) may need to get creative about how to engage in worship settings. Technology can help with this. Worship can be entered into by using recordings of worship music, listening to a podcast, or watching a service online.

Corporate worship can be experienced in a gathering of just a few people—perhaps in a family or a small group. God knows all the circumstances of your life; and when you enter into it with a sincere heart, he will make a way, even if it's creative and nonconventional. Regardless of how you engage in it, worship is central to the practice of keeping the Sabbath.

## SABBATH LIFESTYLE

There is a larger metaphorical understanding of Sabbath—beyond a twenty-four-hour cessation of work—that is conveyed in the New Testament. The writer of Hebrews refers to a "Sabbath rest for the people of God" and encourages followers of Jesus to enter into this rest (see Heb. 4:9–11). The regular experience of Sabbath-keeping seems to foreshadow something bigger than just not working one day a week. It is also an image of stopping our lifetime efforts to be good enough, and instead resting in what Jesus has already done on our behalf. Trying to get into God's good graces by following rules is exhausting! But recognizing that there is nothing more we can do—God has already done it—reminds us of the image of God resting at the conclusion of creation. We too can experience tranquility and peace, knowing that God has provided everything we need for eternal flourishing

Beyond the weekly Sabbath command in Scripture, we see other rhythms of work and rest throughout the Bible. Psalm 104 emphasizes the daily and seasonal rhythms reflected in the pattern of the sun and the moon:

> *He made the moon to mark the seasons,*
> *and the sun knows when to go down.*
> *You bring darkness, it becomes night,*
> *and all the beasts of the forest prowl.*
> *The lions roar for their prey*
> *and seek their food from God.*

*The sun rises, and they steal away;*
    *they return and lie down in their dens.*
*Then people go out to their work,*
    *to their labor until evening. (Ps. 104:19–23)*

We are to work some of the day, and then we are to cease from that work in order to give our bodies rest.

Rhythms of the Sabbath extend beyond the day or even the week. In the Old Testament, God commanded that every seven years there was to be a Sabbatical Year, where the Hebrew farmer was not to sow seeds in his field (Lev. 25:1–7). While some might see this simply as good farming practice, allowing the land to lie fallow periodically, it also had implications for the work life of the farmer and his family. Every seven years, they would rest from their typical annual work of sowing and reaping, and during this year they would trust God to keep the promise of providing for them.

Finally, every fifty years—after seven Sabbatical Years—God instructed his people to celebrate a "Year of Jubilee" (Lev. 25:8–55). Like the Sabbatical Year, farmers were instructed not to plant or harvest during the Jubilee. In addition, this year would allow for a "reset," where all debts would be cancelled and land ownership would revert to the family to which it had originally belonged.[10] While the implications of the Jubilee Year go well beyond rhythms of work and rest, it is clear across various Scriptures in the Old and New Testaments that God cares deeply about our work and our rest.

God intended work and rest to be counterparts to each other in a pattern that could be seen within a given day and through the course of a week, from one season to the next, across the years, and even throughout a person's lifetime. We need to set parameters around the time when work enters our lives. Setting boundaries for our work so that we can rest is necessary. While there may be exceptional times in life where our workload is heavier than normal— parenting a newborn, caring for the sick, or during the occasional intense work season—these should be seen as the exception rather than the rule. Jesus himself embodied this type of exception when he healed a man on the Sabbath. When the Pharisees criticized him for it, he asked them, "If one of you has a child or an ox that falls into the well on the Sabbath day, will you not immediately pull it out?" (Luke 14:5). While there are exceptions, God's design is one of rhythmic consistency.

Some people in some kinds of jobs—those who work the night-shift, seasonal jobs, irregular hours, from home or otherwise—may need to get creative about how and when to practice the Sabbath. Renewal of our minds, hearts, and bodies is available to each of us through the Sabbath. It is a gift, given by a generous God who holds you and your work, each day, in his gracious and capable hands. Will you choose to accept this gift, this week?

## SABBATH STORIES

### Luke's Story

Luke works for a Christian organization in a profession that requires much thinking, writing, and creating resources for others. So for his Sabbath, he refrains from doing what he does Monday through Friday. While each Sabbath looks different, Luke focuses on three words during this time: *diversity*, *liberation* (from a structured 8:00-to-5:00 daily schedule), and *spontaneity*. Luke begins his Sabbath on Friday evening after leaving work, and he enjoys a leisurely pace with his wife that night. They may watch a film, visit friends, or go out to dinner at a favorite Mexican, Italian, or Kansas City BBQ restaurant. A visit with his witty ninety-two-year-old Aunt Glen, who lives in a nursing home, may be part of the agenda some weeks. Other times, a glass of wine and an early bedtime make the list. Contrary to his work life, when Luke practices the Sabbath, there is no set agenda or structure. Leisure is his guiding star.

Saturday morning is reserved for a prolonged Bible study of thirty to forty minutes for Luke. Breakfast is low-key at home, but he and his wife will often go out to lunch or dinner. The emphasis is on something that does not take much time or effort to prepare. From Friday evening through Saturday, Luke avoids the e-mail app on his phone, which connects to his work e-mail account, and he avoids any other technology that is connected with his regular work. Since he is in a profession that requires intellectual labor, he gives his *mind* a rest, which for him means not reading work-related literature.

During warm-weather Saturdays, Luke often spends time in the garage—rearranging items, sweeping the floor, or engaging in a craft. He may mow the lawn, which is an activity that feels relaxing in contrast to his weekly mental work. Luke's Saturday Sabbath time is also reserved for light house cleaning, taking a leisurely warm bath rather than a quick shower, writing personal letters, taking long naps, and listening to music like Earth, Wind, and Fire—all things that can be done at a leisurely tempo. His Sabbath concludes with morning worship at his home church on Sunday. As Luke reflects, "I am not a perfect Sabbatarian," but he is seeking to follow God's commandment, keeping the Sabbath in a way that is consistent with his twenty-first-century life.

### Denise's Story

I grew up in a Christian context where Sunday was set aside for worship, but my family never really talked about the importance of Sabbath rest. I do recall forced naps on Sundays, but in retrospect this was less about my need for rest and more for my parents' benefit. I worked at various jobs through high school and college and was often scheduled for Sunday shifts. I remember my dad sharing his concern that I was burning the candle at both ends, but I chalked it up to parental overprotectiveness. It never occurred to me that my pace of life might be counter to God's plan.

In graduate school and through my early career, I thought of Sunday as the day when I could catch up on all the work I hadn't had time to finish during the week. But shortly after my second child was born, I was exhausted. I was working full time as a professor, had a one-year-old and a newborn, and I was trying to juggle my schedule so we didn't have to put them in daycare.

I had two close friends during this season of life who were also professors—and also the mothers of young children. We talked regularly about our difficulties in trying to get everything done and the lack of margin in our lives. Eventually, because we had been trained as academics, the three of us decided that we would research the topic of "Sabbath." Now, I need to be clear here that all of us knew about the fourth commandment. We were all practicing Christians and had become friends through our workplace at a Christian university. But none of us had ever really practiced Sabbath. Somehow the command to keep the Sabbath seemed more like a good suggestion than a mandate that applied to us.

Over the next several years, we did quite a bit of reading and writing on the Sabbath. We published several academic papers together and co-taught a class on the subject. Along the way, we each began to practice setting aside one day a week when we did not do any work. This turned out to be a good idea, because also along the way I had two more children and I needed that rest!

But the truth was that ceasing from work one day a week was really frightening. I'd always been proud of how much I could accomplish, and the idea of being unproductive for one day out of seven felt sort of wasteful. What if I wasn't able to perform at the same level as before? What if I wasn't prepared for Monday classes or missed deadlines?

Quite surprisingly to me, that did not happen. In what felt like a divine gift, I found that I was never any more behind than I had been before. But what was different was the sense of freedom I had *not* to work on Sundays. Instead I could take a nap (no longer did naps feel forced!). As my kids got older, we used this time to read, play games, or go to the park. I found myself shocked that keeping the Sabbath never seemed to adversely impact my productivity.

My Sabbath-keeping is not perfect, and I have had to think through a number of elements of modern life in the process. Is it okay to go to a restaurant on Sunday? It means I don't have to make a meal, but it means someone else is required to work (my family has decided that this is okay; yours may not). Is it okay to check my e-mail on Sunday? My personal and professional e-mail come to the same inbox, so how should I handle that? What should I do with my smartphone? And so on. Today, I continue to seek God's guidance on these issues. Generally, I use the framework of rest-reflection-relationship to help me determine if any particular activity is helping me better orient to God's purposes for the Sabbath or not.

## THE PRACTICE OF SABBATH

As with most of the practices in this book, you probably won't do this one perfectly the first time you try. Like any habit, the commitment to keep practicing is more important than achieving perfection. One important way to start practicing keeping the Sabbath is to establish a beginning and an ending time. If you haven't practiced a twenty-four-hour Sabbath before, you may want to consider a more bounded time frame—perhaps six or eight hours of time away from "regular" daily distractions. Whatever you choose, plan ahead and prepare. If you don't want to make meals that day, consider using a slow cooker. In order to clear your agenda, you may need to set aside time the day before for additional tasks that would otherwise get in the way.

As you consider what you will "cease" doing, realize that what is labor for one person may not be labor for another. Working in the garden might be toil for the landscaper. But for someone working in an office all week, the same activity might be restful and relaxing. Consider what is life-giving to you—and what is life-draining. Make an effort to do things in the former category and refrain from things in the latter. If you find yourself trying to complete something or identifying tasks you can cross off your to-do list, then you should consider that this might not be the way God wants you to rest. Remember that Jesus was not as caught up in the rules of his day about what activities were or were not permitted on the Sabbath. But this does not negate the idea that the Sabbath is an opportunity for us to stop—to rest from our work, reflect on God's goodness, and engage in relationship with others and with God. We encourage you to keep track of how this practice is going for two or three weeks.

## QUESTIONS FOR REFLECTION OR DISCUSSION

Here are some questions that might help guide some of your reflections:

1. *What are the most significant challenges to you personally in keeping the Sabbath?*

2. *Have you seen examples of others who have engaged in Sabbath practices? Who? What did their experience look like?*

3. *Is it harder for you to work hard for six days or to rest for one?*

4. *What are ways you might be able to build in a more rhythmic experience of work and rest in your life?*

5. *What could your organization do to cultivate healthy rhythms of work and rest?*

# EPILOGUE

## *Paying Attention to God on a Lifelong Journey*

God longs to be in relationship with us in every aspect of our existence. Since we spend a significant portion of our lives working—through paid employment, volunteer work, work in the home, and so on—it is important that we engage with God in our everyday work. Using these spiritual practices is one way to begin to recognize the ways God is working in and through us. Our hope is that this book has provided you with a number of different ways to support and guide your work in the presence of God. Don't be discouraged if you are not able to incorporate every practice outlined in this book on a regular basis. It would be overwhelming to try! Instead, realize that different practices may be more useful in different seasons of life.

The spiritual practices you use depend on your stage of life, work and family demands, personal circumstances, and your needs or desires. You can deepen your relationship with God by embracing the season you are in and selecting a few practices that help you attend to the Holy Spirit's activity in and around you. These practices are meant to be used across a lifetime of work and throughout your various vocations, but they don't all need to be used at the same time. We encourage you to adopt a few with which you have particularly resonated and strive to incorporate them regularly into your working life. When your circumstances change, you may find you need a different repertoire of practices to reinvigorate your working life and your life with God.

Paying attention to God and learning how to be aware of God's presence with us is at the heart of each of these practices. We pray that as you engage in these practices, your awareness of God's movement in your life will grow and your relationship with God will deepen. May you find yourself, as the psalmist did, acknowledging God's presence in every aspect of your everyday life—especially in your work—and may you come to know the voice of the Savior in all things.

> *You have searched me, LORD,*
>> *and you know me.*
> *You know when I sit and when I rise;*
>> *you perceive my thoughts from afar.*
> *You discern my going out and my lying down;*
>> *you are familiar with all my ways.*
> *Before a word is on my tongue*
>> *you, LORD, know it completely.*
> *You hem me in behind and before,*
>> *and you lay your hand upon me.*
> *Such knowledge is too wonderful for me,*
>> *too lofty for me to attain.*
> *Where can I go from your Spirit?*
>> *Where can I flee from your presence? . . .*
> *Search me, God, and know my heart.*
>> (Ps. 139:1–7, 23)

# BIBLIOGRAPHY

Bennett, Kyle David. *Practices of Love: Spiritual Disciplines for the Life of the World*. Grand Rapids: Brazos Press, 2017.

Cosden, Darrell. *The Heavenly Good of Earthly Work*. Grand Rapids: Baker Academic, 2006.

Crouch, Andy. *Culture Making: Recovering Our Creative Calling*. Downers Grove, IL: IVP, 2013.

Erisman, Albert M. *The Accidental Executive: Lessons on Business, Faith, and Calling from the Life of Joseph*. Peabody, MA: Hendrickson, 2015.

Foster, Richard. *Prayer: Finding the Heart's True Home*. New York: HarperOne, 2002.

Harrison-Warren, Tish. *Liturgy of the Ordinary: Sacred Practices in Everyday Life*. Downers Grove, IL: IVP Books, 2016.

Harrower, Scott, and Sean M. McDonough. *A Time for Sorrow: Recovering the Practice of Lament in the Life of the Church*. Peabody, MA: Hendrickson, 2019.

Keller, Tim, and Katherine Leary Alsdorf, *Every Good Endeavor: Connecting Your Work to God's Work*. New York: Penguin, 2014.

Martin, James. *The Jesuit Guide to (Almost) Everything: A Spirituality for Real Life*. New York: HarperOne, 2012.

Messenger, William, ed. *Proverbs*. The Bible and Your Work Study Series. Theology of Work Project. Peabody, MA: Hendrickson, 2014.

Messenger, William, ed. *Theology of Work Bible Commentary*. Theology of Work Project. Peabody, MA: Hendrickson, 2016.

Ortberg, John. *Soul Keeping: Caring for the Most Important Part of You*. Grand Rapids: Zondervan, 2014.

Sandberg, Sheryl. *Lean In: Women, Work, and the Will to Lead*. New York: Knopf, 2013.

Smith, James K. A. *You Are What You Love: The Spiritual Power of Habit*. Grand Rapids: Brazos, 2016.

*Solitude and Contemplation*. Spiritual Practices for Everyday Life Series. Peabody, MA: Hendrickson, 2015.

Willard, Dallas. *The Divine Conspiracy: Rediscovering Our Hidden Life in God*. New York: Harper, 1998.

# NOTES

## PREFACE

1. Tim Keller with Katherine Leary Alsdorf, *Every Good Endeavor: Connecting Your Work to God's Work* (New York: Penguin, 2014), 19.

2. Keller, *Every Good Endeavor*, 22.

3. We are indebted to our friend Dr. Gideon Strauss, academic dean at the Institute for Christian Studies, for the "Wonder, Heartbreak, and Hope" framework of work.

4. As translated by Dr. Terry McGonigal, professor of theology, Whitworth University.

5. Keller, *Every Good Endeavor*, 76.

6. Sophia Smith, "The Japanese Art of Recognizing Beauty in Broken Things," *Make*, accessed September 7, 2017, https://makezine.com/2015/08/17/kintsugi-japanese-art-recognizing-beauty-broken-things.

7. Darrell Cosden, *The Heavenly Good of Earthly Work* (Grand Rapids: Baker Academic, 2006), 197.

8. Andy Crouch, *Culture Making: Recovering Our Creative Calling* (Downers Grove, IL: IVP, 2013), 212.

## INTRODUCTION

1. Dallas Willard, *The Divine Conspiracy: Rediscovering Our Hidden Life in God* (New York: Harper, 1998), 61.

2. Tish Harrison-Warren, *Liturgy of the Ordinary: Sacred Practices in Everyday Life* (Downers Grove, IL: IVP Books, 2016), 99.

3. "Biography of Brother Lawrence Illuminates Prayer," *Intermountain Catholic*, accessed February 19, 2019, http://www.icatholic.org/article/biography-of-brother-lawrence-illuminates-prayer-3831830.

4. From *Sacred Ordinary Days*, https://sacredordinarydays.com.

5. Kyle David Bennett, *Practices of Love: Spiritual Disciplines for the Life of the World* (Grand Rapids: Brazos Press, 2017).

6. Kristen Deede Johnson, "Are We Missing the Point of Spiritual Disciplines?," *Christianity Today* online (August 18, 2017); emphasis added.

## CHAPTER 1

1. James K. A. Smith, *You Are What You Love: The Spiritual Power of Habit* (Grand Rapids: Brazos, 2016), 99.

2. Smith, *You Are What You Love,* accessed February 19, 2019, http:// englewoodreview.org/james-k-a-smith-you-are-what-you-love-feature -review/.

3. Warren, *Liturgy of the Ordinary*, 108.

4. For more information on *A New Liturgy*, visit http://www.anew liturgy.com.

5. *Pray as You Go*, https://pray-as-you-go.org/.

## CHAPTER 2

1. In the 1800s, the German rabbi Samson Hirsch wrote that the *mezuzah* is a way of "hallowing the house . . . as an abode where G-d is ever present and where the service of G-d is fulfilled." Samson Raphael Hirsch, *Horeb: A Philosophy of Jewish Laws and Observances*, trans. Dayan Dr. L. Grunfeld, 7th ed. (London: Soncino Press, 2002), 59.

## CHAPTER 3

1. John Ortberg, *Soul Keeping: Caring for the Most Important Part of You* (Grand Rapids: Zondervan, 2014), 134.

2. "Walk Slow and Carry Questions," *The Next Right Thing* podcast, episode 16, https://emilypfreeman.com/wp-content/uploads/2017/11 /Episode16.pdf.

3. Denise Daniels, "A Management Professor's Perspective on Work in the Bible," https://www.theologyofwork.org/resources/a-management -professors-perspective-on-work-in-the-bible.

## CHAPTER 4

1. For more on the concept of fixed mindset versus growth mindset, see Carol S. Dweck, *Mindset: The New Psychology of Success* (New York: Ballantine Books, 2007).

2. *The Bible Experience* (Grand Rapids: Zondervan, 2007), CD Audio.

3. In some workplaces, people gather weekly to read or listen to Scripture out loud, which can be an even more powerful experience. See www .publicreadingofscripture.com for an app and other resources.

4. *Pray as You Go*, https://pray-as-you-go.org.

5. Cory Willson, "Poetics of Everyday Work: A Neo-Calvinist Approach to Vocational Discipleship in Local Churches" (PhD diss., Fuller Theological Seminary, 2015), 175 and 211.

6. The Theology of Work Project has developed the Bible and Your Work Study Series that discusses workplace issues. Each lesson is designed to be done in a half hour (such as during a lunch break or over breakfast before work). There is also a complete *Theology of Work Commentary*, which provides details of Scripture that pertain to work. For more information, visit www.hendrickson.com.

7. William Messenger, ed., *Proverbs*, Theology of Work Project, The Bible and Your Work Study Series (Peabody, MA: Hendrickson, 2014), 6.

## PART TWO

1. Keller, *Every Good Endeavor*, 22.

## CHAPTER 5

1. Doug Koskela, *Clarity and Calling: Discovering What God Wants for Your Life* (Grand Rapids: Eerdmans, 2015), 54.

2. Ibid.

3. Ibid.

4. The initial conversation between Moses and God is found in Exodus 3–4. However, the rest of the book of Exodus continues this conversation that started in the early chapters.

5. Pierre Teilhard de Chardin, "Patient Trust," *Hearts on Fire*, accessed September 27, 2018, https://www.ignatianspirituality.com/8078 /prayer-of-theilhard-de-chardin.

## CHAPTER 6

1. Colin Powell (BrainyMedia, 2019), accessed April 25, 2019, https:// www.brainyquote.com/quotes/colin_powell_386437.

2. Lara Casey, "Cultivate What Matters," www.cultivatewhatmatters .com.

3. Sheryl Sandberg, *Lean In: Women, Work, and the Will to Lead* (New York: Knopf, 2013).

4. Albert M. Erisman, *The Accidental Executive: Lessons on Business, Faith, and Calling from the Life of Joseph* (Peabody, MA: Hendrickson, 2015), 93.

5. For a wonderful explanation of how this can be played out, listen to Tim Keller's sermon on Esther, "If I Perish, I Perish," https://gospelinlife .com/downloads/esther-and-the-hiddenness-of-god.

6. Erisman, *The Accidental Executive*, 91.

7. Robert A. Emmons and Michael E. McCullough, "Counting Blessings versus Burdens: An Experimental Investigation of Gratitude and Subjective Well-Being in Daily Life," *Journal of Personality and Social Psychology* 84, no. 2 (2003): 377–89.

8. Nancy Digdon and Amy Koble, "Effects of Constructive Worry, Imagery Distraction, and Gratitude Interventions on Sleep Quality: A Pilot Trial," *Applied Psychology: Health and Well-Being* 3, no. 2 (2011): 193–206.

9. Patrick Hill, Mathias Allemand, and Brent Roberts, "Examining the Pathways between Gratitude and Self-Rated Physical Health across Adulthood," *Personality and Individual Differences* 54, no. 1 (January 2013): 92–96.

10. Lisa A. Williams and Monica Y. Bartlett, "Warm Thanks: Gratitude Expression Facilitates Social Affiliation in New Relationships via Perceived Warmth," *Emotion* 15, no. 1 (2014).

11. C. Nathan DeWall, Nathaniel M. Lambert, Richard S. Pond, Todd B. Kashdan, and Frank D. Fincham, "A Grateful Heart Is a Nonviolent Heart: Cross-Sectional, Experience Sampling, Longitudinal, and Experimental Evidence," *Social Psychological and Personality Science* 3, no. 2 (2012): 232–40.

12. Amit Kumar and Nicholas Epley, "Undervaluing Gratitude: Expressers Misunderstand the Consequences of Showing Appreciation," *Psychological Science* (2018).

## CHAPTER 7

1. For the full story, see 2 Samuel 11–12.

2. "Alan Mulally: Producing Cars with Passion and Involvement," *Ethix* (July 15, 2010), https://ethix.org/2010/07/15/producing-cars-with -passion-and-involvement.

3. See Andy Molinsky, "The Five Key Ingredients of an Effective Apology," *Psychology Today* (May 7, 2018), https://www.psychologytoday.com/us /blog/adaptation/201805/the-five-key-ingredients-effective-apology.

# CHAPTER 8

1. For a fuller discussion, see Margaret Diddams and Denise Daniels, "Good Work with Toil: A Paradigm for Redeemed Work," *Christian Scholar's Review* 38, no. 1 (2008): 61–82.

2. This story can be found in the book of Job. Throughout the book, Job is in conversation with his friends, who provide their own explanations for his misfortune. Job rejects their explanations, and much of his response to them can be understood as a lament to God.

3. In *A Time for Sorrow: Recovering the Practice of Lament in the Life of the Church*, edited by Scott Harrower and Sean McDonough (Hendrickson, 2019), six scholars/pastors trace the role of lamentation in the Old and New Testaments, reflect on the theological significance of lament, affirm the ongoing relevance of lamentation in the church, and explore its biblical roots and application in church practice.

# PART THREE

1. Annie Dillard, "The Writing Life," accessed February 19, 2019, https://www.brainpickings.org/2013/06/07/annie-dillard-the-writing-life-1/.

# CHAPTER 9

1. To explore this practice further, see *Solitude and Contemplation* in the Spiritual Practices for Everyday Life series (Peabody, MA: Hendrickson, 2015).

2. Ull Chi, "Life in the Intersection" (personal journal entry, 2011), printed with permission. Poetry adaptation from T. S. Eliot, *Ash Wednesday*.

# CHAPTER 10

1. James Martin, SJ, *The Jesuit Guide to (Almost) Everything: A Spirituality for Real Life* (New York: HarperOne, 2012), 97.

2. Richard Foster, *Prayer: Finding the Heart's True Home* (New York: HarperOne, 2002), 28.

3. Martin, *The Jesuit Guide to (Almost) Everything*, 88–89.

4. Ibid., 11.

5. Foster, *Prayer*, 27.

6. Foster, *Prayer*, 30.

7. Cf. James Martin's discussion of "the grace to know my sins," in *The Jesuit Guide to (Almost) Everything*, 89.

8. For a season, Richard Foster prayed the Prayer of Examen while shooting the basketball in the driveway. See Foster, *Prayer*, 34.

9. Martin, *The Jesuit Guide to (Almost) Everything*, 89.

10. Many of the questions in each section of the examen are taken or adapted from "Examen for Managers," http://www.ignationsprituality.com/ignatian-prayer/the-Examen/review-of-the-day-for-managers.

## CHAPTER 11

1. Lydia Saad, "The '40-Hour' Workweek Is Actually Longer—By Seven Hours," *Gallup News* (August 29, 2014), http://www.gallup.com/poll/175286/hour-workweek-actually-longer-seven-hours.aspx.

2. Richard Swenson, "Tackling Torque," *Life at Work* 2, no. 4 (July/August 1999).

3. Jeffrey M. Jones, "In U.S., 40% Get Less than Recommended Amount of Sleep," *Gallup News* (December 19, 2013).

4. Jessica Dickler, "Workers Use Only about Half of Their Vacation Time," *CNBC Careers* (May 24, 2017), https://www.cnbc.com/2017/05/24/workers-use-only-about-half-of-their-vacation-time.html.

5. The early Christians adopted Sunday as their day of worship in celebration of Jesus' resurrection.

6. Eugene Peterson, "The Pastor's Sabbath," *Leadership* (Spring 1985): 55–56.

7. Peterson, 56.

8. A number of research studies in the social sciences support these findings. See the following for more in-depth coverage of these phenomena: Bert Uchino, *Social Support and Physical Health: Understanding the Health Consequences of Relationships*, Current Perspectives in Psychology (New Haven: Yale University Press, 2004); Kenneth I. Pargament, *The Psychology of Religion and Coping: Theory, Research and Practice* (New York: Guildford Press, 1997); Daniel N. McIntosh, Roxane Silver, and Camille B. Wortman, "Religion's Role in Adjustment to a Negative Life Event: Coping with the Loss of a Child," *Journal of Personality and Social Psychology* 65 (1993): 812–21.

9. Willard, *The Divine Conspiracy*, 61–62.

10. Unfortunately, there is no evidence that the Israelites ever followed the command to celebrate the Year of Jubilee.

# About the Hendrickson Publishers/Theology of Work Line of Books

There is an unprecedented interest today in the role of Christian faith in "ordinary" work, and Christians in every field are exploring what it means to work "as to the Lord" (Col. 3:22). Pastors and church leaders, and the scholars and teachers who support them, are asking what churches can do to equip their members in the workplace. There's a need for deep thinking, fresh perspectives, practical ideas, and mutual engagement between Christian faith and work in every sphere of human endeavor.

This Hendrickson Publishers/Theology of Work line of books seeks to bring significant new resources into this conversation. It began with Hendrickson's publication of the *Theology of Work Bible Commentary* and other Bible study materials written by the TOW Project. Soon we discovered a wealth of resources by other writers with a common heart for the meaning and value of everyday work. The HP/TOW line was formed to make the best of these resources available on the national and international stage.

Works in the HP/TOW line engage the practical issues of daily work through the lens of the Bible and the other resources of the Christian faith. They are biblically grounded, but their subjects are the work, workers, and workplaces of today. They employ contemporary arts and sciences, best practices, empirical research, and wisdom gained from experience, yet always in the service of Christ's redemptive work in the world, especially the world of work.

To a greater or lesser degree, all the books in this line make use of the scholarship of the *Theology of Work Bible Commentary*. The authors, however, are not limited to the TOW Project's perspectives, and they constantly expand the scope and application of the material. Publication of a book in the HP/TOW line does not necessarily imply endorsement by the Theology of Work Project, or that the author endorses the TOW Project. It does mean we recognize the work as an important contribution to the faith-work discussion, and we find a common footing that makes us glad to walk side-by-side in the dialogue.

We are proud to present the HP/TOW line together. We hope it helps readers expand their thinking, explore ideas worthy of deeper thought, and make sense of their own work in light of the Christian faith. We are grateful to the authors and all those whose labor has brought the HP/TOW line to life.

William Messenger, Executive Editor, Theology of Work Project
Sean McDonough, Biblical Editor, Theology of Work Project
Patricia Anders, Editorial Director, Hendrickson Publishers

www.theologyofwork.org
www.hendrickson.com